Land Law
2023/2024

Simply Notes

CONTENTS

WHAT IS THIS BOOK?

1. It is a **simple and straightforward introduction to land law**.
2. It is an **up-to-date set of land law subject notes**. The law is stated as up-to-date on 1st August 2023.
3. It is a book designed to give you a **quick and accessible knowledge of land law for your particular course of study**, before you move on to more complex texts. Would I recommend moving on to more complex texts? Yes, always. What would I recommend? Well, I'm afraid I'm a little bit old school and recommend *Grey and Grey, Elements of Land Law*. It's a great book, both in the sense that it is huge – the current edition has nearly 1,500 pages – but it is also a great book in the sense that it is comprehensive and detailed. I do have one reservation about *Grey and Grey*, and that is that it was last published in 2008. That's 15 years of law which is not covered in the most recent edition. So, if you want a more current in-depth text, I recommend *McFarlane, Hopkins, and Nield, Land Law: Text, Cases and Materials*. That book is detailed, provides extracts from cases and scholarly works, and will certainly take your understanding of land law to the next level.
4. It is suitable for students studying **LLB or combined honours degree**, **Graduate Diploma in Law (GDL)**, **Postgraduate Diploma in Law (PGDL)**, **LLM/MA law conversion courses**, **Solicitors' Qualifying Examination 1 (SQE 1)**, or **CILEx** qualifications.
5. It is a book which is **not a replacement for hard work and dedication to the programme of study** you have embarked on.

WHAT DO I WANT FROM YOU?

One thing. Just one thing: A bit of feedback would be great. I have developed this book in response to the feedback received from the first edition which was published in 2018/19. I have introduced tables, diagrams, and changed explanations, all in response to feedback. Feedback works, especially where it is constructive, so a bit of constructive feedback would be nice. Of course, I have ideas for the next edition, which will look different to this edition, but you, the students of land law who have taken a punt on this book and will use it, you will be able to tell me better than anyone else what works, what's okay but needs to be tweaked, and what needs improvement, even overhaul. So, take time to complete the survey when Amazon sends you the link and I will thank you daily until the next edition is published. Emoji time: 😊🔥👍, and *thank-you.*

CHAPTER 1
INTRODUCTION TO LAND LAW

Introduction: What is land law all about?

1.01 Land Law is all about rights: Identifying rights; creating rights; and, protecting rights, in relation to land. The rights which exist in relation to land vary greatly, with some being more significant than others; some are major, and some are minor. The methods by which these rights can be created also vary, with some requiring strict formality (which usually means some form of writing), while other rights can be created informally by the behaviour of the parties.

1.02 As if this weren't (seemingly) complicated enough, there are schemes of protection for these rights which might, ultimately, mean whether the rights are binding on, ie, enforceable against, others. However, this wider picture is for later in the book. The first stage in understanding land law, is understanding the **definition of land**.

What is land? How is it defined?

1.03 It is important to know what constitutes 'land' before considering other parts of land law. An adequate definition of land is valuable because it sets down the extent of an individual's rights over property. However, a definition of land is also important for the tax man (who can levy stamp duty) and the mortgagee (a bank or building society) who might repossess the land.

Statutory Definition

1.04 Section 205(1)(ix), Law of Property Act 1925 contains a definition of 'land'. The definition, which is not exhaustive, states that land *includes* land of any tenure (freehold or leasehold), mines and minerals, buildings or parts of buildings and other corporeal hereditaments; also rent and other incorporeal hereditaments, and easements, rights, privileges, or benefits relating to land.

1.05   These are the key elements of the definition, but let's put it into plain language – what does it mean? Land law is about the buildings we can see, the trees, and the rivers, but it is also about the things we cannot see *but* which can also be interests in land, eg, rights of way, mortgages, and all the other things necessary to make land useful. So, land is tangible, it is physical, but land is also intangible, it is not physical, but is nevertheless meaningful and valuable.

1.06   Now, the definition, while it is helpful, isn't everything we need in order to understand the definition of land. For the rest, we need to look at the common law.

Above and Below the Ground

1.07   The basic common law position is rather crudely summed up by the Latin maxim *cuius est solum eius est usque ad coelum et ad inferos* – he who owns the land, owns everything below the land and everything above it up to the heavens. However, this maxim is only part of the story and doesn't accurately reflect the law.

Above the Ground

1.08   A landowner does not enjoy ownership of all the space above their land. The extent of their enjoyment is **limited to that which is necessary for the ordinary use and enjoyment of the land** and any structures on it. The distinction is between the lower and upper strata of airspace; the lower is the landowner's (**Kelsen v Imperial Tobacco Co (1957)**), the upper is not (**Bernstein of Leigh (Baron) v Skyviews & General Ltd (1978)**).

1.09   In **Kelsen v Imperial Tobacco Co (1957)**, an advertising sign projected a few inches into the airspace above the landowner's shop. This was held to interfere with the landowner's property rights and a court ordered its removal from the airspace. Similarly, in **Laiqat v Majid (2005)**, an extractor fan was erected which projected 75cm into the landowner's garden at a height of

4.5m, also had to be removed as it was a trespass. Even moveable items such as cranes oversailing land can be said to have committed trespass and actionable (**Woolerton & Wilson v Richard Costain Ltd (1970)**).

1.10   Now, you might be sitting there and thinking – but what harm was done? Well, it is frequently the case that no harm is done, but that is not the point. An action in trespass, the tort which forms the basis for these claims, does not require the claimant to prove they have suffered loss or damage by the trespass. To put it in the technical language. Trespass is **actionable *per se***, that is, without proof of loss or damage.

1.11   The cases in paragraph 1.09 can be contrasted with **Bernstein of Leigh (Baron) v Skyviews and General Ltd (1978)**, where the defendant flew over the landowner's property and took photographs to sell to the residents. The landowner claimed it was a trespass, but given it was high above the land, it was not a trespass.

1.12   But, I hear you ask, can we put a figure on it? Is there a limit to the lower stratum and up to that point I can call it my own? Well, yes, there probably is a limit, but we take as our guide a set of regulations imposed on aircraft. These are the Rules of the Air Regulations 2007 SI No 734 which provides, in Schedule 1, regulation 5(3)(b), that an aircraft shall not be flown within 500 feet of a person, vessel, vehicle, or structure. Now, for those who like the metric system, that is about 152 metres. Problematically, these regulations were revoked by the Rules of the Air Regulations 2015 (SI 2015/840) which make no reference to a 'low flying' level or 500 feet. However, it is worth bearing the 2007 regulations in mind, even though revoked, since they are a useful guide.

1.13   So, it might be sensible to regard 500 feet or 152 metres as the limit of the lower strata and any entry into that space above your house would likely be an actionable trespass. Now, of course, that is easier to prove with an overhanging sign, an air conditioning unit, or the branches of a tree (**Lemmon v Webb (1894)**) than it is with an aircraft flying across your land. But, if you can prove it, then an action *may* be successful, subject to the next point.

1.14   As a postscript to this discussion, it should be noted that 76(1), Civil Aviation Act 1982, gives immunity from trespass or nuisance where the aeroplane is sufficiently high above ground, accounting for the weather, etc, as is reasonable. What does this mean? Well, an aircraft in typical flight conditions could not commit trespass, and it may be able to fly lower, into the lower stratum, if weather conditions render it, in all circumstances, reasonable to fly at that level.

1.15   So, the limits of what you can claim belong to you above your land are, sadly, limited. As **Bernstein of Leigh (Baron) v Skyviews and General Ltd (1978)** reminds us, it is what is reasonably necessary for the ordinary use and enjoyment of land.

Below the Ground

1.16   If you own some of the space above your land, it must also follow that you own some of the land below. The starting point is that a land owner will enjoy the right to anything which is under the land they own **(Waverley BC v Fletcher (1996))**, unless there is a statutory or common law rule which takes it from him!

1.17   Minerals and other similar substances *generally* form part of the estate of the landowner and he is able to treat them as his own. However, coal belongs to the Coal Authority (Coal Industry Act 1994) and oil and natural gas to the Crown (Petroleum Act 1998).

1.18   The Crown, by prerogative, has the right to mines of gold and silver. In addition, where items found are classed as treasure under the Treasure Act 1996, these vest in the Crown.

1.19   All other items found below the ground of the landowner belong to the landowner. In **Waverley BC v Fletcher (1996)**, the defendant, while on council land, found a medieval brooch approximately nine inches below the surface. The coroner held that it was not treasure trove, so the question of ownership arose. The CA held that the brooch belonged to the council.

Treasure

1.20   All treasure vests in the Crown, therefore it is necessary to determine its definition. The starting point for the modern law is the Treasure Act 1996 ("TA 1996"). Now, this act is horribly drafted – if you don't believe me take a look at section one – which is bewildering on first read. So, let me unpick it for you. Treasure is as follows:

i. Any object, not a coin but, for example, a brooch, at least 300 years old with 10% precious metal by weight;

ii. One of at least two coins in the same find, at least 300 years old, with at least 10% precious metal;

iii. One of at least 10 coins in the same find and at least 300 years old, but not necessarily being of precious metal;

iv. An object at least 200 years old of a class designated by the Secretary of State;

v. An object regarded as treasure trove under the old law, but not in the definition in the Treasure Act 1996;

vi. Any object, of whatever precious metal, found in the same place or previously had been with another object that is treasure.

1.21   In 2023, the definition of treasure was expanded by the Treasure (Designation) (Amendment) Order 2023, amending an earlier 2002 Order, to include objects, any part of which, is metal, and which are at least 200 years old and meet a specified threshold of historical, archaeological, or cultural significance. The definition is designed to respond to problems generated by some finds, notably Roman, which would not previously have met the definition of treasure because they were either made from bronze or non-precious metals.

1.22   Now, 'precious metal' is central to the definition, so what does it mean? Well, the definition is quite narrow and limited to gold or silver (s3(3), TA 1996). This causes problems for object finds which might be otherwise regarded as treasure but lack a precious metal element. It is this problem which the government hopes to address by a proposed reform to the law (see para 1.23, below).

1.23   Where treasure is found, it vests in the Crown (s4(1)(b),

TA 1996). Under the Act, a person who finds an object which *he believes or has reasonable grounds for believing is treasure* (s8(1)), must notify the coroner within 14 days beginning with the day after the find was made (s8(2)(a)). If later, it is the day on which the finder first believes or has reason to believe the object is treasure (s8(2)(b)). Failure to report is a criminal offence, punishable by three months' imprisonment or a fine (s8(2)(a) and (b)), unless the finder is able to demonstrate a reasonable excuse for failing to notify the coroner (s8(4)). Where the coroner determines the item(s) found constitute treasure, then a reward may be paid (s10(2)).

Items found on the ground

1.24   The best claim to items found on the land is the claim of the true owner of the item. So, in **Moffat v Kazana (1969)**, a home owner purchased a house and found cash in an old biscuit tin which had been hidden in the wall, but which became dislodged when work was carried out. The previous house owner claimed the tin and its contents and the court upheld the claim despite the current homeowner, and finder, claiming the tin as his due to it being found on what was now his land.

1.25   But what if the true owner cannot be identified? Well, the person with the better claim is the finder of the item who can prove a better claim against any person, except the true owner (**Armory v Delamirie (1722)**). Of course, if the true owner comes forward, then they must return the item.

1.26   If the owner of the land on which the item was found is able to demonstrate an intention to exercise control over the area, then this may be sufficient to mean that the landowner can claim an item found over the claim of the finder. In **Parker v British Airways Board (1982)**, a bracelet was found in the British Airways executive lounge at Heathrow. The finder handed it to BA staff, left his contact details, and left. BA could not find the owner, so sold the bracelet. The finder sued claiming the bracelet. In finding for the finder, the CA held that as the item had been lost or abandoned, and the finder took possession of the item, they had a better claim than everyone except the true owner unless the occupier of the area manifested an intention to exercise control over the building and the things found on it. Since they did not have the requisite control, the finder had an action in damages for the loss.

Fixtures and Chattels

1.27   One of the most examinable areas is that of fixtures and chattels because it has, for something apparently so simple, caused such stress for home buyers, lenders (mortgage-providers) and others. A solid starting point is the basic idea that **a fixture is part of the land**, so passes to a buyer when the land is bought. A **chattel is a moveable object and does not form part of the land but can be taken away by the seller** when they move out.

1.28   When does the distinction matter? It matters in a number of different scenarios, and one has been identified above, namely when a house is being sold. When a **house is being sold**, the buyer wants to know what makes up the land they are buying, while the seller wants to know what they can take away with them when they move out. However, it is also relevant when the **mortgage company wants to sell the house** after the borrower has defaulted, that is, not paid their mortgage for a number of months. In that case, the mortgage company wants to know what forms part of the land when they sell it, and what is a chattel and belongs to the borrower since these calculations will affect the price. It is also relevant at the **end of a lease** since fixtures belong to the landlord, while chattels belong to the tenant. Finally, whether something is a fixture or a chattel affects the value of the land and, therefore, the level of stamp duty which HMRC can levy on the sale. So, as can be seen, fixtures and chattels raises itself as an issue in a number of situations.

1.29   Before going into the relevant law, one final point is worth noting. In a sense, this is a bit of a reality check. When a house is being sold, which is the most common platform for a fixtures-chattels dispute, the seller completes a form, which is part of the standard conveyancing process, indicating what will stay and what will move with the seller. This greatly reduces the scope for dispute, but it does not remove it entirely. Mistakes can be made, and where they are made, then the common law rules step in to resolve it. So, let's take a look at the common law rules.

When is a chattel not a chattel? When it's a fixture

1.30   The common law developed two tests to determine the status of an item: The **degree of annexation test** and the **purpose of annexation test**. While both remain relevant to the modern law, the latter test is the preferred test.

Degree of Annexation Test

1.31   The degree of annexation test states that the more firmly an object is fixed to land or to a building, the more likely it is to be a fixture. It follows from this that if the item is under its own weight, then it is a chattel, unless there is a contrary intention that it is meant to be a fixture. In **Holland v Hodgson (1872)**, from which these statements of law come, spinning looms bolted to the floor of a factory were held to be fixtures. Likewise, central heating systems, lifts, an alarm system and swimming pool filtration plant were held to be fixtures in **Melluish v BMI (No 3) Ltd (1996)**. An air conditioning system recessed into the walls of a building was also a fixture in **Aircool Installations v British Telecommunications (1995))**.

1.32   By contrast, where machinery was resting under its own weight, it was regarded as a chattel in **Hulme v Brigham (1943)**, and a movable greenhouse was also held to be a chattel in **HE Dibble Ltd v Moore (1970)**.

(b) Purpose of Annexation Test

1.33   As indicated, the **purpose of annexation** is the primary test (**Hamp v Bygrave (1983)**) and the one which might rebut the degree of annexation test. The test asks: Is the item fixed for the more convenient use of the item as a chattel, or for the more convenient use of the land? If the former, it's a chattel, even if tightly fixed. If the latter, it's more likely to be a fixture. The purpose of annexation is viewed objectively (**Botham v TSB Bank plc**

(1997)).

1.34 Therefore, in **D'Eyncourt v Gregory (1866)**, stone garden ornaments standing under their weight were held to be fixtures because they were part of an architectural design. Their *purpose* was the improvement of the land and not to enjoy the items as chattels. It should be noted from this case that the items were not fixed so the degree test might have regarded them as chattels and capable of being removed, but the purpose trumped degree test. In **Berkley v Poulett (1977)**, on the other hand, a statue and sundial resting under their weight were held to be chattels as they were there for their aesthetic value, not as part of an overall design. The purpose was to enjoy them as items, and not to make overall improvements to the land. This was also the position in the case of **Tower Hamlets London Borough Council v Bromley London Borough Council (2015)**, where a Henry Moore statue could be removed and sold since it was resting under its own weight and not part of a design scheme to a housing estate, despite being part of a local authority policy of promoting works of art in public places.

1.35 In **Leigh v Taylor (1902)**, tapestries securely fixed to a wall were held to be chattels because they had to be fixed to be enjoyed. The *purpose* of annexation was to enjoy them as tapestries, despite the degree of annexation indicating that they were fixtures. By contrast, in **Re Whaley (1908)**, the fixing of tapestries to the walls was part of the overall design scheme of an Elizabethan manor house. Therefore, they were regarded as fixtures because the *purpose* was to enhance the land which was an Elizabethan manor.

1.36 The law continues to evolve in this area and following the case of **Elitestone Ltd v Morris (1997)**, the courts consider the ease with which an item can be removed and the objective intention behind the placing of the item. Where removal of the item is only possible by destruction of it, by causing some form of damage, then it will be regarded as a fixture and could not be removed. In this respect, the case of Elitestone is instructive.

1.37 In the case of Elitestone, Morris lived in a bungalow on land owned by Elitestone. The bungalow stood on the land under its own weight, but was on concrete posts. Elitestone wanted to redevelop the land and sought to remove Morris, and others, from their bungalows. Morris resisted the claim on the basis that he lived in a 'dwelling house' for the purposes of the Rent Act 1977 (since repealed) and was therefore a protected tenant who could not be removed from the land. The House of Lords found in favour of Morris. The bungalow, despite not being physically attached (fixed) to the land, was part and parcel of the land. It could not be removed from the land without demolishing or damaging it. It was objectively intended to be there for purposes of occupation and, as such, was intended as a fixture, despite the absence of a physical attachment to the land.

1.38 Where property can be removed without destruction of damage, it will be outside the Elitestone case. Therefore, in **Mew v Tristmire (2011)**, a houseboat was held to be a chattel, despite connection to services, because it could be removed without destruction. Likewise, in **Caddick v Whitsand Bay Holiday Park Ltd (2015)**, a holiday bungalow was held to be a chattel as it could be removed without destruction. Of course, a holiday bungalow could also be distinguished from the permanent dwelling nature of the bungalow in Elitestone, since a holiday bungalow is not meant for permanent occupation and the owners would have an alternative dwelling.

CHAPTER 2
ESTATES AND INTERESTS IN LAND

Introduction

2.01   This chapter, and the chapter which follows it, are *probably* the most important chapters in this book. The reason is that, between them, they cover the fundamentals of land law: Estates and Interests and how they are acquired (chapter two), and protection of interests once created (chapter three). These chapters are long, certainly when compared to other chapters in this book, so take some time to learn the material in them, and to understand it, and land law should make a whole lot more sense.

2.02   Now, before I go on, a health warning: Just when you think you have it with land law, it will throw up an exception to the general rule you just understood. So long as you understand when these exceptions to the general rule operate, land law settles down once again and becomes relatively straightforward. With that in mind, let's start thinking about fundamentals: **Legal and Equitable Rights**, **Estates in Land**, and **Interests in land**.

Legal and Equitable Rights

2.03   Over the coming chapters and pages, you will read a lot about legal and equitable rights. At times, you may be thinking, and I would have some sympathy, *'what's the point?'* Well, the answer is historical, as it is for a lot of land law. In England, as the legal system developed, two court systems developed. On the one hand, there were **courts of common law**, while on the other hand, there were **courts of equity**. Both courts had the authority to hear disputes on the same facts, but could frequently give different decisions and found different points of law. This is why, today, we have legal rights, developed by the common law courts, and equitable rights, developed by the courts of equity. These rights remain in English land law today, the principal difference being that they are determined by one court structure.

2.04   Yes, it is frustrating to have estates and interests, some of which are legal, some of which are equitable, and some of which are both! Nevertheless, the points have been rationalised somewhat so it is a bit easier and slightly more straightforward to understand than might have been the case 150 years ago. So, that is some consolation for you, even if it only feels like tiny consolation at the moment. Still, don't worry, I'm here to guide and that is what I will do.

2.05   I'll leave you with this final thought on the legal-equitable rights distinction as a hoped-for point of clarification. It is this: Broadly, whether an interest is legal or equitable depends, to a large extent, on how the interest has been created, which we will consider in this chapter, and protected (registered) which we will consider in chapter three. With that thought in your mind, let's move on to the other key elements of land law and start with **Estates in Land**.

Estates in Land

2.06   An estate in land is the period a person enjoys the rights associated with their land. Since 1st January 1926, there have been **two estates in land which are capable of being legal** (s1(1), Law of Property Act 1925). Note, these estates in land are *capable* of being legal, meaning they could also be equitable. Whether they are legal or equitable depends on how the interests were created, but more on that later. For now, let's stick to estates.

2.07   The two estates in land under the Law of Property Act 1925 are the **freehold estate** (or to give its formal title, the **fee simple absolute in possession**)(s1(1)(a), LPA 1925) and the **leasehold estate** (its formal title being the **term of years absolute**)(s1(1)(b), LPA 1925).

2.08   Now, I will explain what these fancy-sounding titles mean in a moment, but before I do, another fundamental: **we do not own the land, we own the *title* to the land**. Why? Well, I answer that question next.

Not ownership of land – Ownership of title

2.09   We own the title to land, not the land. That is fundamental. The reason is historical. After the Norman Conquest of England in 1066, land ownership was reformed so that all land was owned by the Crown. All others owned rights as *tenants* of the Crown providing services in return. This system was, to a degree, abolished in the 17th century. Today. the Crown remains owner of the land, while folk like us own a title to an estate. So, we should refer to ownership of title, but does this mean that we always do it? No. Lawyers, especially land lawyers, get lazy. We still talk about land ownership because it's familiar and everyone understands us, but when we want to make correct statements of *land ownership*, we should say that it is ownership of title to an estate.

2.10   As indicated, above, there are two estates in land: freehold and leasehold. These two estates are both, technically, periods of ownership in land. Of these two, the freehold estate is the closest English law comes to awarding ownership of *land*. This is because when we hold title to a freehold estate, it can be held by me and my successors forever, that is as long as there are people able to inherit the title it will keep going. By contrast, the leasehold estate, as its name suggests, is a lease. Leases come to end by the passage of time because they are time-limited.

2.11   Since we have made all that clear, now would be a good time to delve a little more deeply into these two estates in land.

Freehold Estate

2.12   As indicated, the freehold estate is known technically as the **fee simple absolute in possession**. This definition needs to be broken down to be understood. The **fee** part means that it is inheritable, and the **simple** element means that the inheritance is not limited to a particular individual. The **absolute** element means that the freehold is not subject to any conditions which might bring it, prematurely, to an end. Finally, the **possession** element has it that the current holder of the freehold has the current right to enjoyment of the property associated with the freehold.

2.13 The freehold estate is **capable of being legal**. What does the *capable* bit mean? This means that it will **only be legal** if it is **created** and **protected in the correct way**. This requires the transfer to be **completed by deed** (s52, LPA 1925). A deed is a document which is **signed by the grantor** (the 'grantor' is the person who executes the deed), **witnessed, delivered** (meaning, **dated**), and **states on its face that it is a deed** (s1, Law of Property (Miscellaneous Provisions) Act 1989). If this has been done, it has been **created** in the correct way.

2.14 The second stage is that it must also be **protected** in the correct way. In other words, the new title holder must be registered as the new owner of the land under ss4(1) and 27(1), Land Registration Act 2002. Once this is done, the new freeholder has a valid legal freehold estate in land. The issue of protection is discussed in detail in Chapter Three.

2.15 If the freehold title is sold, there is a further stage which needs to be completed, and this is before the deed and registration stages, and that stage is the **contract stage**.

'Contract Stage'

2.16 Generally, contracts have no formalities in English law, which you will know from your study of contract law. However, that is subject to exceptions, and a notable one relates to land. A **contract for the sale of land** made on or after 27th September 1989, must comply with the requirements of s2, Law of Property (Miscellaneous) Provisions Act 1989.

2.17 Section 2, LP(MP)A 1989 requires that a valid contract for the sale of land must be:

    (i)   in writing;

    (ii) contain all the terms; AND,

    (iii) be signed by both parties

2.18   The requirement of writing speaks for itself. The document may be a single document containing all the terms which is signed by both parties, or it may be two identical documents which are signed, then exchanged by, both parties.

2.19   A document which proposes to vary the terms as originally agreed must comply with s2 (**McCausland v Duncan Lawrie Ltd (1996)**), but the document itself may incorporate its terms by reference to another document (s2(2)).

2.20   When it comes to the signature, it would usually be the recognised hand-written signature of the parties, but **Neocleous v Rees (2019)** permitted the automatic footer 'signature' at the end of an email to count as signature for the purposes of a section 2 contract. While this decision is only a County Court decision, it does demonstrate a clear movement towards electronic creation and execution of land documentation, especially in light of two factors. First, moves to electronic conveyancing and, secondly, the impact of the pandemic on the way legal documents were executed when face-to-face meetings were prohibited.

2.21   Though the previous discussion relates to contracts for the sale of land, s2, LP(MP)A 1989 also needs to be satisfied in other situations, eg, options to purchase, rights of pre-emption, etc. These are highlighted and discussed later. Note, also, that s2 does not apply in some other scenarios, eg, purchase of land at public auction, or to situations where an implied trust arises (s2(5), LP(MP)A 1989).

2.22   A reminder of the stages of a land transaction:

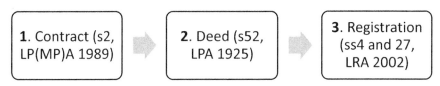

Leasehold Estate

2.23   The leasehold estate is the other **estate in land *capable* of being legal**. Note, as with the freehold estate, it is only capable of being legal if it is created and protected in the correct way, but more on that later.

2.24 The technical name or the leasehold estate is the **term of years absolute**. It is a '**terms of years**' because a leasehold estate must be for a certain, but limited, period of time. So long as the term is certain, that satisfies the requirement. A term could be 999 years, 10 years, five years, two years, and so on. It is also the case that a term of years can be for a period of *less than a year*, eg, for six months. This is still a term of years because it falls within the statutory definition of a terms of years (s205(1)(xxvi), LPA 1925).

2.25 It is absolute because the leaseholder's rights are not subject to conditions and can only be brought to an end, for example, by the expiration of the term, that is, by passage of time. An example of a conditional lease which would *not* be absolute is one which ends when the leaseholder reaches a certain age. This would be rare.

2.26 In order to be a valid leasehold estate, the interest claimed must have the **characteristics of a lease**. In **Street v Mountford (1985)(HL)**, it was said that a lease has three characteristics. First, it must have a **certain term**; secondly, it must give the tenant **exclusive possession**; and, thirdly, it must charge a **rent**. However, s205(1)(xxvii), LPA 1925 does not list rent as a requirement, which was taken to be the position in **Ashburn Anstalt v Arnold (1989)(CA)**. However, most leases would require the payment of rent. Let's consider these characteristics of a lease in more detail.

Certain term

2.27 A lease must be for a fixed period of time, having a certain start date and a certain end date. Thus, a lease for the 'length of the war' was not valid in **Lace v Chantler (1944)**, nor one for a period until the land was needed by the landlord for development purposes, as in **Prudential Assurance Co Ltd v London Residuary Body (1992)**.

2.28 Where the term is not set at the start of the tenancy, this may be valid as a lease on a **periodic tenancy** basis. That is, if payment of rent is monthly, then it will be a **monthly periodic tenancy**, or paid annually, then an **annual periodic tenancy (Prudential Assurance Co Ltd v London Residuary Body (1992))**. Both would be valid because they have a certain term, ie, the period for whatever the rent is paid.

Exclusive possession

2.29   A tenant must have exclusion possession of the property. This means the right to exclude others from the property, including the landlord.

2.30   Where a claimed leasehold estate does not have the characteristics of a lease, then it will not be a lease, but may be something else. For example, it may be a **licence**. A licence is a **mere permission** to be on the land but **it is not a property right**.

2.31   The issue of exclusive possession was one which used to be litigated significantly in the past because of landlords desperately trying to avoid the protections given to tenants under a lease. This happens less often nowadays because the key statute which afforded tenants protection, the Rent Act 1977, has been repealed. That said, proving a lease or a licence may still arise as an issue when it comes to remedies and so on.

Leasehold Estate: Capable of being legal

2.32   This is an estate in land which is *capable* of being legal. Again, it is only *capable* of being legal, meaning if it is not *created* and *protected* in the correct way, **it will not be legal, but *may* be equitable**.

2.33   Every lease of **more than three years** must be **created by deed** (s52, LPA 1925; s1, LP(MP)A 1989). Whether it is *protected* in the correct way will depend on the length of the lease. If it **is lease of more than seven years**, it must be **substantively registered** (s27(2)(b)(i) Land Registration Act

2002). Substantive registration means that it is treated as its own separate estate and should get its own title number at the Land Registry. If the lease is **not more than seven years**, it is **protected automatically** without the need for registration (sch3, para1, LRA 2002). This means they would automatically bind a new owner of the freehold title. This is discussed in more detail in Chapter Three.

2.34   In the previous paragraph, I mentioned that leases of more than three years must be by deed. But what, I hear you ask, about leases of three years or less? Well, earlier, it was mentioned that in some circumstances land law creates exceptions to its general rule, and this is the first one. A legal lease can be created informally, ie, without a deed, so long as it is **not longer than three years**, takes effect **in possession**, and for **'best' rent**, ie, market rent, without payment of a premium (s54(2), LPA 1925). This is a legal lease, even though there is no deed, and it is protected because it overrides under sch3, para 1, LRA 2002, as explained in 2.33, above.

2.35   If the lease is not created or protected in the correct way, then it may be a **legal period tenancy**, if it complies with s54(2), LPA 1925, or, as is also possible, an **equitable lease**.

Equitable Lease

2.36   An equitable lease can arise in a number of ways. First, as stated, it can arise because an attempted legal lease fails; secondly, only a s2, LP(MP)A 1989 agreement to create a lease has been agreed; or, thirdly, the person granting the lease has only an equitable lease themselves, so can only grant an equitable lease. In the first and second situations, so long as the document complies with s2, LP(MP)A 1989, see paras 2.16 – 2.21, above, it will be a valid equitable lease. In the third situation, it only needs to have signed writing to be valid (s53(1)(a), LPA 1925). This different statutory requirement in the third scenario is reflected in the fact that the lease can only have been equitable from the outset. This is what is sometimes referred to as an **inherently equitable interest** because it could *never* be legal.

2.37   An equitable lease is protected in registered title by a

Notice on the Charges Register of the registered freehold (s32, LRA 2002). Where the freehold title is unregistered, then the equitable leaseholder protects their interest by registering a C(iv) land charge (s2(4), Land Charges Act 1972). This is discussed in more detail in Chapter Three.

Legal Interests in Land

2.38   We have looked at the estates in land, but land law is about more than the estates. Land cannot be used as well as it might be without a whole range of other, lesser, interests. These interests are wide-ranging, and, like estates in land, they can be **legal** or **equitable**. Let's start with those interests which are *capable of being legal*. There are three which are important for our purposes, so they are mentioned; the others are of only minor significance.

2.39   The interests in land which are **capable of being legal are contained in s1(2), LPA 1925**. The first is **easements and profits** (s1(2)(a), LPA 1925). An easement is the right enjoyed over your neighbour's land, eg, a right of way over your neighbour's land. A profit is the right to take something from another's land, eg, firewood from woodland on someone else's land. Easements are an important interest in land and discussed in detail in Chapter Five.

2.40   The second interest capable of being legal is a **charge by way of legal mortgage** (s1(2)(c), LPA 1925). In plain English, a **mortgage**, which is a loan of money secured by a charge over the borrower's property. This is another important interest in land and is discussed in more detail in Chapter Six.

2.41   Finally, the third interest which is capable of being legal is a **landlord's right of entry** (s1(2)(e), LPA 1925), which allows the landlord to enter to terminate a lease, or enter to enforce a rent charge. These are discussed in more detail in Chapter 11.

2.42   In order for these interests to be legal, they must be created and protected in the correct way. First, they must satisfy the requirements of the provision. For example, an **easement**, to be **legal**, must be for the **length of a freehold or a leasehold estate** (s1(2)(a), LPA 1925). Secondly, it must then be created by

deed, see para 2.13, above. Thirdly, and finally, the interest may need to be registered to be protected. As the particular interests are protected in different ways, you will see that in the relevant chapters to come, I have explained how the particular interests are discussed in the context of that particular interest.

2.43   Once again, if the conditions are not met in some way, then the interest **will not be legal**, but it *may* **be equitable**.

Equitable Interests in Land

2.44   All other interests not listed in s1(2), LPA 1925 will be equitable (s1(3), LPA 1925). The most common equitable interests are **restrictive covenants** (Chapter Four), **beneficial interests under a trust** (Chapters Eight and Nine), and **Estate Contracts**. It is worth saying a little more about estate contracts.

2.45   An estate contract is an equitable interest in land. It is, in essence, a contractual right and includes important rights such as **options to purchase** and **rights of pre-emption**. An **option to purchase** is the **right to purchase land when the buyer decides to purchase it**. Sometimes, options to purchase are time-limited, that is, the option can only be exercised within, say, 12 months of being created. A **right of pre-emption** is linked to an option to purchase, but the onus is on the seller. When the seller decides to sell their land, they must offer it to the holder of the right of pre-emption first, before they offer it to others.

2.46   The **contract stage of a land contract** is also an **estate contract**. Equity will give the remedy of specific performance once the contract stage is met because of the maxim *equity looks on as done that which ought to be done*. This means that the seller will have to execute a deed to transfer legal title once a valid estate contract for the sale of land has been executed. The estate contract under a land purchase contract may be protected by registration as a notice in the Charges Register where title to the estate is registered (s32, LRA 2002), or as a C(iv) land charge where title to the estate is unregistered (s2(4)(iv), LCA 1972). This is discussed in more detail in Chapter Three.

2.47 The formalities for the creation of an equitable interest are, generally speaking, dependant on the **type of equitable interest**. As indicated, **estate contracts** need to comply with **s2, LP(MP)A 1989**, whereas interests such as **equitable easements** and **restrictive covenants**, need only comply with **s53(1)(a), LPA 1925 (signed writing)**. A **beneficial interest under a trust which is expressly created** must comply with **s53(1)(b), LPA 1925**, meaning that it must be **evidenced by signed writing**, whereas a **beneficial interest under an implied trust** is **not subject to formalities (s53(2), LPA 1925)**. This is discussed in detail in Chapter Nine.

CHAPTER 3
REGISTERED AND UNREGISTERED TITLE

REGISTERED TITLE: Introduction

3.01   In the previous chapter, we looked at the formalities for the creation of interests. We saw that for a legal interest, generally, a deed should be executed (s52, LPA 1925), whereas for equitable interests either an estate contract (s2, LP(MP)A 1989) or signed writing will be enough (ss53(1)(a) and (b), LPA 1925). However, that is no longer enough in English land law. English land law requires you to jump through one more hoop. That hoop is registration of the estate or interest on a central register so that it is binding on anyone who buys the land.

3.02   Since the 19th century, there have been many attempts to create a single and comprehensive register of all titles and the interests in it for land in England and Wales. The latest is the Land Registration Act 2002 ('LRA 2002') which replaces the Land Registration Act 1925. Registration is, as its name suggests, the requirement that if you want to keep your interest so that you can prove it and bind third parties, then you register your estate or interest on the register. This should, it is thought, simplify land purchase and avoid the need for the paper chase which existed previously. So, on that footing, let's start our look at land law by examining the rationale for registration before looking at the detail of registration.

Rationale of Registration

3.03   A system of registration of title where all ownership interests are provided in one place, accessible to the public, makes good sense for a number of reasons. First, it provides external evidence of ownership and limits the chances of loss occurring because of the loss of key documents. Secondly, it allows land to be bought and sold more easily, without the need to investigate ownership interests over lengthy and sustained periods. Thirdly, it promotes efficiency and transparency in land ownership, at least in theory.

3.04 Underpinning the rationale for registration are the **Principles of Registered Title: Mirror Principle, Curtain Principle, and Insurance Principle**.

3.05 The **Mirror Principle** is the idea that the register should *reflect*, fully, all the interests which exist in respect of title to land. This allows a buyer, who wants to buy a piece of land, to understand all the rights which exist in or over the land which he wishes to buy. It also allows the buyer to say that if the interest was not on the register before they bought it, then they should not be bound by it. As you will see over the next few pages, it is not the case that the register reflects all the interests in the land.

3.06 The **Curtain Principle** is a loose metaphor. The law allows a buyer not to worry about beneficial interests which might exist under a trust of land by drawing a curtain over them. Therefore, the buyer is entitled to worry about only the people in front of the curtain, the legal owners, and not those behind the curtain, the beneficial owners. So long as the buyer pays the purchase money to two trustees or a trust corporation (a company which manages a trust), then he will defeat the beneficial interests under the trust of land. This is known as overreaching and the governing law is in ss2 and 27, LPA 1925. Overreaching is an important aspect of any land purchase and is discussed in more detail later.

3.07 Finally, the **Insurance Principle**, which is essentially a guarantee by the state, through the Land Registry, as to the accuracy of the Register. If the register is inaccurate and an individual suffers loss as a result of the inaccuracy of the register, then the state will compensate the victim. The provision of insurance is logical given that the state requires that the register be used to protect estates and interests in land and that failure to register can lead to loss of the right claimed. So, at least the register is guaranteed to encourage use.

Format of the Register

3.08   We now turn attention to the format of the register. Now, there is the first misleading statement. The register is not *one register*, rather it is *three registers*. The three registers are the **Property Register**, **Proprietorship Register**, and the **Charges Register**. They each perform a different function in the registration of estates and interests in land. Each is dealt with in turn.

3.09   The **Property Register** is that part which describes the land by reference to a plan, which is frequently an Ordnance Survey map where the land is outlined in red pen. However, the Land Registry does not regard the map as definitive. The Property Register also outlines the rights which benefit the land.

3.10   The **Proprietorship Register** provides the name and address of the proprietor (the owner), the nature of the title (ie, whether it is freehold or leasehold), and whether there are any restrictions affecting the owner's ability to deal with the property. For example, there might be a restriction indicating that there is a beneficial owner of the property and that the Land Registry may decline to register a new legal owner until the restriction is addressed.

3.11   Finally, the **Charges Register** lists the rights which burden the land, eg, they will say that the land has a restrictive covenant placed on it which limits what the owner can do with the land, such as, not run a business from the land or, if it is a bungalow, not to build a second storey on the house.

What attracts protection on the register?

3.12   There are three categories of registerable interests:

(i) Registered Estates – There are two estates which are to be registered: (a) Fee simple absolute in possession (freehold estate); and, (b) Term of Years Absolute of <u>more than seven years</u> (leasehold estate).

(ii) Registered Charges – mortgages.

(iii) Other Registerable Interests – Restrictive Covenants; *some* Easements; Options to Purchase; and, a Spousal Right of Occupation. Under s32, LRA 2002, these should be protected by entry as a Notice on the Charges Register of the burdened estate. Failure to register an interest gives rise to a loss of priority with the result that it will not bind a purchaser.

Restrictions on the Proprietorship Register

3.13   Sometimes there will be some restriction or limitation on the owner's ability to deal freely with their property (s40, LRA 2002). These limitations will be registered literally as a 'restriction' on the Proprietorship Register. The classic example is requirement that in order to defeat a beneficial interest under a trust of land, the 'capital' monies should be paid to two trustees or a trust corporation. This is known as overreaching and is explained at the end of this chapter. A restriction may be indefinite, for a fixed period, or until the occurrence of an event. A restriction operates as a 'warning light' to a potential purchaser. In order to proceed, the Land Registry will need to be satisfied that the *warning light is turned off.*

Notices on the Charges Register

3.14   Most interests, as indicated, will be protected by this method. Notices might either be unilateral or agreed, but in any event the holder of the benefit must register the notice against the title of the burdened land. What does this mean? Well, let me explain with an example. Albert and Bob are next door neighbours. Albert agrees a covenant with Bob so that Albert agrees not to run a business from his land. This is a restrictive covenant because it *restricts* Albert's use of his land. In order to protect this interest against a buyer of Albert's land, Bob, whose land benefits from that covenant, will need to register the covenant against Albert's (burdened) land. By registering a **Notice on the Charges Register** (s32, LRA 2002) of the burdened land (Albert's land), notice of the restrictive covenant is provided to any buyer of Albert's land so they *know that there is a restriction on the use of the land* if they buy it. That is part of the purpose of the register. It allows a buyer to see the rights which will affect the land they plan to buy.

3.15 Failure to register an interest by notice when it ought to have been means the holder of the interest suffers a loss of priority against a purchaser for valuable consideration (s29, LRA 2002). Note, entry of a notice does not mean the interest is valid; that is a separate question of law. Registration is only concerned with protection. So, going back to Albert and Bob and the restrictive covenant they agreed, if Bob does not register that before Albert sells his house to Cassie, Cassie will not be bound by the restrictive covenant and could run a business from the land. So, registration is important because it protects the rights you claim to have been given! The moral of the tale of Albert, Bob, and Cassie is, *if you can register your interest, register your interest to protect it!*

3.16 Some interests cannot be protected by Notice on the Charges Register. These interests are the interests of a beneficiary under a trust of land (s33(a), LRA 2002), a lease of three years or less (s33(b), LRA 2002) and, a covenant agreed between a landlord and tenant (s33(c), LRA 2002). While this may seem odd, these can be protected in other ways. These are discussed later.

Interests which Override

3.17 The idea behind title registration is to ensure a complete and accurate register of all interests in or over land. You will remember that this is summed up in the 'Mirror Principle'. However, there is one significant exception to this under the LRA 2002 and it is **interests which override**. These are interests which *may be* binding on a purchaser, yet do not appear on the register. Hayton (1981) described them as a 'crack in the mirror'.

3.18 But why is it that these interests bind? Well, they are broadly important rights and they can, in the general scheme of things, be found in other ways, that is, by wandering around the property and identifying that, just maybe, someone else occupies the land which is for sale, possibly under a short lease. So, they are not totally obscure and impossible to find, they simply require more effort to identify them. It is also frequently the case that the rights protected this way are created informally and, because of that, it may not be reasonable to expect them to be registered.

3.19 Under the LRA 2002, the list which is currently identified as overriding will be reduced to a handful of key rights. That has not happened yet, so there are still some fairly obscure rights on it. That being said, I will focus on the main ones. These are the ones which your land law module will inevitably focus on, so they are the ones you need to know. They are: (i) **leases of seven years or less**; (ii) **interests which override by actual occupation**; (iii) **implied legal easements**.

(i) Leases of seven years or less

3.20 Where the lease is a legal lease for a term of seven years or less, it will override under sch 3, para 1, Land Registration Act 2002. So, these short leases cannot be registered. If you tried to register your short lease, the Land Registry would decline to register it. Remember, leases of more than seven years must be substantively registered.

3.21 The rationale behind this is to stop the register being clogged up with lots of short leases. Imagine a situation where the law requires leases of 12 months, six months, or even one month to be registered. There would be a steady stream of registrations and the register would become impossible to administer and the work of the civil servants would be increased. So, it is sensible to keep these off the register.

(ii) Interests of those in actual occupation

3.22 This is the most significant of all the overriding interests. This is the one which will come up most often in your questions on registration. The law is contained in sch 3, para 2, Land Registration Act 2002 and associated case law. To establish that your interest is one which binds by actual occupation, the person claiming the right has to show that they have an interest capable of binding – *actual occupation is not a right in itself* – and protect it by being in actual occupation of the land. So, remember...

What is 'an interest'?

3.23   First, the interest must be a property right, and a mere licence will not satisfy this requirement (**Strand Securities v Caswell (1965)**). This was confirmed by the Supreme Court in the case of **Scott v Southern Pacific Mortgages Ltd (2014)**. **Interests** which might be protected by *actual occupation* under sch 3, para 2, LRA 2002:

Beneficial interest under a trust	**William's & Glyn's Bank v Boland (1981)**
Equitable leases	**Grace Rymer Investments Ltd v Waite (1958)**
Estate contracts	**Bridges v Mees (1957)**
Options to purchase	**Ferrishurst Ltd v Wallcite Ltd (1999)**
Rights of pre-emption	**Kling v Keston Properties Ltd (1983)**

3.24   Note, a **spousal right of occupation** is *not* an interest which will override by actual occupation (s30(10)(b), Family Law Act 1996) since it is not a property right.

What is 'actual occupation'?

3.25   Once the claimant has identified an *interest*, they must demonstrate that they were also in **actual occupation** in order to protect the interest.

3.26   Actual occupation is a question of fact but interpreted by use of ordinary words of plain English (**Williams & Glyn's Bank v Boland (1981)**). In terms of what the courts are looking for, it is '*some degree of permanence and continuity*' (*per* Lord Oliver in **Abbey National v Cann (1991)**), the *intentions and wishes of the party*, the *period of absence from the property and the reason for the absence, together with the personal circumstances of the person* (**Link Lending v Bustard (2010)**).

3.27   Putting this into practice, the easiest cases are those where the person claiming their interest is protected by actual occupation are *actually living in the property*, as in **Williams & Glyn's Bank v Boland (1981)**.

3.28   More difficult are those cases where there are **periods of absence from the property** and whether these negative actual occupation. In such cases, the general approach is whether the party has an *intention to return to the property*. For example, in **Chhokar v Chhokar (1984)**, a wife's absence from the property while giving birth did not undermine her claim that her interest was protected by actual occupation when her husband sold the house and made off with the sale money. Similarly, in **Link Lending v Bustard (2010)**, Bustard was subject to an involuntary detention in a psychiatric hospital away from her home, but kept furniture at the property and had her post sent to it indicating an intention to return. Therefore, the court held that she was in actual occupation of the property.

3.29   By way of contrast, in the case of **Stockholm Finance Ltd v Garden Holding Inc (1995)**, a Saudi princess, who had never set foot in the property, could not claim to be in actual occupation by proxy where a cleaner visited the flat from time-to-time, or where another attempted to give the flat a 'lived-in look' by switching on lights, setting a burglar alarm, watering plants, and running the central heating system. None of these activities amounted to actual occupation. This is consistent with a line of cases where occupation through a third party is insufficient unless they are a caretaker in a formal *caretaking* role (**Strand Securities v Caswell (1965)**). The key question being *why* the representative (caretaker) is in occupation. If there merely to *keep an eye on things*, then this is not likely to be sufficient for actual occupation (**Pennistone Holdings Ltd v Rock Ferry Waterfront Trust (2021)(CA)**).

3.30   Where an individual claims an interest in the whole of a piece of land, but is in actual occupation of only part of it, then the interest will only override for that part of the land.

3.31   These cases are principally concerned with residential claims to actual occupation, whereas it is also possible for commercial claims to be protected by actual occupation. For example, in **Malory Enterprises Ltd v Cheshire Homes (UK) Ltd (2002)**, the storage of goods and the erection of a perimeter fence on derelict land was evidence of actual occupation, while in **Blacklocks v JB Developments (1982)**, the erection of a barn on farmland was sufficient to establish actual occupation. Another common example of actual occupation may also be parking on a regular basis (**Kling v Keston Properties Ltd (1983)**).

Will the interest always be protected where actual occupation is proven?

3.32   What would happen if an interest is established and the party claiming protection is successful in showing they are in actual occupation? Well, it will not always be protected. This is because there are two exceptions written into schedule 3, paragraph 2, LRA 2002 which provide that a purchaser will not be bound by an overriding interest if **the interest is not disclosed on reasonable inquiry** or **it belongs to a person whose occupation would not have been obvious on a reasonable inspection of the land**.

(iii) Implied legal easements

3.33   Implied legal easements override under schedule 3, paragraph 3, Land Registration Act 2002. Express legal easements and all equitable easements must be registered as a Notice on the Charges Register. This is discussed in detail in chapter five.

UNREGISTERED TITLE: Introduction

3.34   The registered system of estates and interests in land is the dream of land law. However, there remains a system which we call the **unregistered** system of protection which is different to the one we have just discussed and which protects interests differently. This was the scheme which operated before the register was available in all areas of England and Wales.

What do we mean by 'unregistered'? What is unregistered?

3.35   By *unregistered*, we mean that the principal title to the estate in land is not registered. The owner of that estate proves their title to land by **producing the title deed**. This is literally by the production of a piece of paper proving that the title to the land belongs to them. Ownership is not recorded in a single register, but must be investigated by different means.

3.36   Now, here is the spanner in the works. Despite the fact that the principal estate is **not registered**, there is a *limited scheme which permits interests against that estate to be registered*. For example, the holder of the benefit of a restrictive covenant will be able to register the benefit against the name of the holder of the unregistered estate on a register called the **Land Charges Register**. The governing statute is the Land Charges Act 1972.

3.37   So, to be clear, the unregistered system does not have a main registered estate, ownership by the estate owner is proved by holding the title deeds. By contrast, people with interests in or against *that* estate, eg, an easement or restrictive covenant, can register that interest against the name of the estate owner on the Land Charges Register. Note, this is not the same register as in registered title. They are different systems, with different registers.

Legal and Equitable Interests

3.38   Importantly, before we go on, it should be flagged that once more the legal and equitable interest difference is crucial to understanding *how* the different interests are protected. Let's start with **legal interests** because they are most straightforward: **Legal interests bind the whole world**. What does this mean? Well, it means that these interests are binding on a purchaser of the *unregistered* estate without the need for registration. So, if you have a legal easement, it would be binding on the unregistered estate even though *it is not* and *cannot* be registered.

3.39   On the other hand, **equitable interests** are a little bit more complicated in that they fall into three categories:

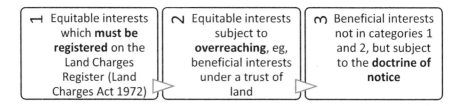

| 1 Equitable interests which **must be registered** on the Land Charges Register (Land Charges Act 1972) | 2 Equitable interests subject to **overreaching**, eg, beneficial interests under a trust of land | 3 Beneficial interests not in categories 1 and 2, but subject to the **doctrine of notice** |

3.40   We will deal first of all with the equitable interests which must be registered. This is the limited scheme of registration under the Land Charges Act 1972. All of the equitable interests listed, and one *legal* interest, must be registered as a **land charge**. The land charges have a letter and number classification.

3.41   The odd-one-out, that is, the legal interest which must be registered, is the **puisne mortgage**. A puisne (pronounced *puny*) mortgage is a second mortgage granted in unregistered title. This has to be registered because a first legal mortgage would take custody of the legal estate titleholder's title deeds as security.

Category One: Equitable interests which must be registered (Land Charges Act ('LCA') 1972)

3.42   Under the Land Charges Act 1972, certain interests will only be protected if they are registered. Once registered, the interest is binding on a purchaser; if not registered, the interest will be **void** against a purchaser depending on the *type of purchaser*. The LCA 1972 envisages two types of purchaser: (i) a **purchaser for valuable consideration** (which includes marriage consideration) and (ii) a **purchaser for money or money's worth** (which is something which might be quantified in monetary terms so excludes marriage consideration).

3.43   Under the limited scheme of registration, there are six classes of interest: Class A, B, C, D, E and F. The main interests will be considered. If you want them in easy table form, here you go, before they're discussed in detail:

Interest	Land charge
Estate Contract	Class C(iv) land charge
Restrictive Covenant	Class D(ii) land charge
Equitable Easement	Class D(iii) land charge
Spousal Right of Occupation	Class F land charge
Puisne Mortgage	Class C(i) land charge

Class C (iv) land charge – estate contract

3.44   Under s2(4)(iv), LCA 1972, estate contracts should be registered as a class C (iv) land charge. Examples of an estate contract include an option to purchase, or a right of pre-emption, etc. Failure to register this land charge renders the interest **void against a purchaser of the *legal* estate for money or money's worth** (s4(6), LCA 1972).

Class D (ii) land charge – restrictive covenant

3.45   A restrictive covenant is an agreement to limit the use of land, eg, not to build an extension. This interest is an equitable interest. Failure to register this land charge renders the interest

void against a purchaser of the *legal* estate for money or money's worth (s4(6), LCA 1972). Covenants created before 1st January 1926 are still governed by the doctrine of notice. These are still relevant, so it is worth bearing this in mind.

Class D (iii) land charge – equitable easements

3.46   An equitable easement is one which has not been created by deed, or is not for the length of either of the legal estates in land. Failure to register this land charge renders the interest **void against a purchaser of the *legal* estate for money or money's worth** (s4(6), LCA 1972). As with restrictive covenants, this only relates to equitable easements created since 1st January 1926. Equitable easements created earlier are still subject to the doctrine of notice.

Class F land charge – Family Law Act 1996

3.47   This is a right of occupation available to a spouse whose name is not on the legal title. This is not an interest in land, rather a mere statutory right of occupation. Failure to register this land charge renders it void against a **purchaser of *any* interest for valuable consideration** (s4(5) and (8), LCA 1972).

Category Two: Equitable interests subject to overreaching, eg, interests under a trust of land

3.48   Overreaching is the process by which an interest in land is removed and turned into an interest in the purchase money paid by the buyer of the land. For overreaching to occur, the purchase monies must be paid to two trustees or a trust corporation. This is concerned with interests which are quantifiable in monetary terms, eg, an interest under a trust of land. Overreaching is discussed later.

Category Three: Equitable interests not in categories one and two, subject to the doctrine of notice

3.49 Those interests not in categories one and two are dependent for their enforceability on the **doctrine of notice**. These are:

(i) Interests excluded by the LCA 1972, ie, pre-1926 equitable easements and restrictive covenants, and covenants between landlord and tenant.

(ii) A beneficial interest under a trust where overreaching has not occurred.

(iii) Mere equities.

(iv) Interests arising by estoppel.

3.50 If a purchaser wishes to take a property free of any equitable interests, then he must demonstrate that he is a bona fide purchaser for value of a legal estate without notice: This is the essence of the **doctrine of notice**. This means that he must be a good faith purchaser of the legal estate providing valuable consideration (including marriage consideration) **without notice** of the equitable interest. There are three types of **notice**:

(i) **Actual notice** – where the purchaser has actual knowledge of a third-party interest (s198(1), LPA 1925);

(ii) **Constructive notice** – where the purchaser can be taken to know of the existence of an interest, but does not ask questions which mean they would obtain further information about the interest;

(iii) **Imputed notice** – this is notice obtained by the purchaser's agent, eg, a solicitor during the course of the purchase (s199(1)(ii)(b), LPA 1925).

Overreaching

3.51 This concept scares most students of land law, but is actually a very simple idea. When purchasing property, the purchaser would be better advised that land free of equitable interests under a trust will be more valuable. Therefore, he will want to ensure that when purchasing property, the purchase rids the land of any equitable interest under a trust – this is done by the **process of overreaching**. Overreaching takes the equitable interest off the land and transfers it into an equitable interest in the purchase money paid by the purchaser. This balances the interests of a purchaser who will wish to take the land free of equitable interests under a trust, and the person with the interest who at least receives monetary compensation in the form of the purchase price.

3.52   The statutory provisions which relate to overreaching are ss2 and 27, Law of Property Act 1925. This stipulates that overreaching occurs where the conveyance (payment of purchase monies, or payment of mortgage monies) is made to at least two trustees or to a trust corporation.

3.53   The two leading cases on overreaching are **Williams & Glyn's Bank Ltd v Boland (1981)** and **City of London Building Society v Flegg (1988)**.

3.54   In *Boland*, a wife contributed to the purchase price of the property, but the property was registered in the husband's name alone. So, even though not the registered legal owner, the wife had an equitable interest under a presumed resulting trust (**Bull v Bull (1955)**). Subsequently, the husband mortgaged the property to the claimant bank, and failed to maintain the repayments. The question arose as to whether the bank was bound by the wife's equitable interest. It was held that a mortgage was a qualifying conveyance for the purposes of overreaching, but that in failing to pay the mortgage monies to two trustees, the bank took the house subject to the wife's interest as a person with an interest in actual occupation.

3.55   In contrast, in *Flegg*, parents, a daughter and son-in-law purchased a house together. The parents provided half the purchase price, but the house was registered in the joint names of the daughter and son-in-law. Some time later, the daughter and son-in-law mortgaged the property to the City of London Building

Society. When they defaulted on the loan, the issue of the rights of the parties arose. The parents claimed an overriding interest in actual occupation under s70(1)(g), LRA 1925. However, the building society successfully argued that as the mortgage monies had been paid to two persons under s2, LPA 1925, the interests of the parents had been overreached and the building society took the property free of their interest.

3.56   It is important to note that **overreaching operates in the same way** whether title to the land is unregistered or registered.

3.57   Such is the effect of overreaching that so long as the conditions for its operation are met, the buyer need not worry about the nature of any beneficial interests under a trust asserted by a third party, even where the buyer knew about the beneficial interest under the trust (**N3 Living Ltd v Burgess Property Investments Ltd and another (2020)**).

3.58   Well done for sticking with the last two chapters. They are the building blocks of land law and it is difficult to **get** what land law is about without them. Okay, so you may not get it immediately, and you'll have to go back and forth to chapters two and three for the rest of your study of land law – _every_ student does – but the key thing is that you understand their importance to your success on this module. To emphasise their importance and to provide a reminder, throughout the rest of this book, I flag the relevant bits on creation and registration when we look at the specific interests which exist in land. So, that's what we'll now do over the following chapters. Strap in!

CHAPTER 4
FREEHOLD COVENANTS

Introduction

4.01 In English law, freehold owners may agree with another to do, or not to do, something in relation to their land. Such agreements are known as **covenants**. A covenant to do something, eg, to maintain a boundary fence, is a **positive covenant**; a covenant not to do something, eg, not to use a property for business purposes, is a **restrictive (or, negative) covenant**.

4.02 When the original parties agree to something, all covenants agreed between them are enforceable, whether they are positive or negative, as a matter of basic contract law. However, problems start in English law when the land subject to the covenant is sold to a new owner and the question arises as to **whether covenants can be enforce by, or against, a new owner**. Here, we look at questions of the rules at **common law** and the rules in **equity**, since both treat covenants differently. However, before we start on that, it's useful to understand the terminology.

4.03 The problem is explained in diagram form:

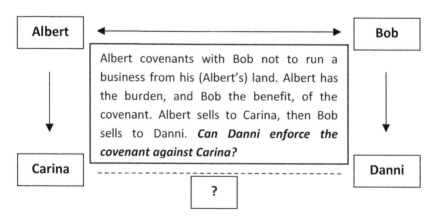

Albert covenants with Bob not to run a business from his (Albert's) land. Albert has the burden, and Bob the benefit, of the covenant. Albert sells to Carina, then Bob sells to Danni. *Can Danni enforce the covenant against Carina?*

4.04 As the diagram, above, demonstrates, between Albert and Bob, the agreed covenant is enforceable as a matter of contract law. But what about when Albert sells the burdened land to Carina, and Bob sells the benefited land to Danni? **Will Danni be able to enforce the covenant against Carina?** In other words, **has the burden of the covenant agreed by Albert passed to Carina on sale to her? AND, has the benefit of the covenant agreed by Bob passed to Danni on sale?** That is the essence of the problems generated by freehold covenants. The next few pages will all be about whether the benefit and burden can pass to the new owner.

4.05   One final point before we get into the detail. This is an area where, once again, there are different rules at common law and in equity. We saw in 2.03 – 2.04 how English law had two systems of administering justice: common law and equity. We also saw that they developed different rules and these different rules are very evident in land law. Well, perhaps nowhere else in English land law is this more obvious than in freehold covenants.

4.06   Now, if you don't want to know the answer, look away now! Or, as is the more modern expression, here is a ***SPOILER ALERT***. I can answer everything you need to know about the enforceability of covenants in one line before I go on to explain it in detail across the coming pages. So, if you don't want the simple answer, skip the rest of this paragraph. Put simply, the position is as follows: **Covenants are not enforceable against a successor in title (new owner) of the original burdened land at common law, while in equity, only restrictive (negative) covenants are enforceable against a successor in title (new owner) of the original burdened land**. That is the general position. I will now discuss the detail for those who love that sort of thing.

Terminology

4.07   Before we get into it, some definitions. There is some tricky terminology to get straight in your head before we discuss the depth. A covenant is a **promise contained in a deed**. The parties to the covenant are known as the **covenantor** and the **covenantee**. The party who **makes the promise**, that is, **takes**

the burden, is the **covenantor**; the party who receives the promise, ie, **takes its benefit**, is the **covenantee**. The **burdened land**, ie, the land of the **covenantor**, is sometimes referred to as the **servient land**; the land which has the **benefit**, ie, the land of the covenantee, is sometimes referred to as the **dominant land**.

Original parties

4.08　Now, as already stated, the original parties can agree to any covenants, positive or negative, and they will be enforceable between them as a matter of contract law. Problems start when the original covenantor sells their land and this raises a question. We have explained this, but rehearsal of it can do no harm: **Can the new owner of the burdened land have the covenants enforced against them?** Also, when the original covenantee sells their land, this raises the question: **Can the new owner of the dominant land enforce the covenants against the current owner of the burdened land?**

4.09　As indicated earlier, there are clear differences between the common law rules and the rules in equity. We will now look at the rules in detail to determine whether the covenants can be enforced by and against new owners of the land. We'll start with the common law rules.

Common Law (Benefit)

Will the benefit of a covenant pass to a new owner of the dominant land at common law?

4.10　The short answer to this question is 'Yes', provided it is by one of the following methods: (i) Express Assignment; (ii) the conditions from P&A Swift Investment v Combined English Stores (1989) have been met; (iii) Contract (Rights of Third Parties) Act 1999; (iv) s56, Law of Property Act 1925.

(i) Express Assignment

4.11   Under s136, Law of Property Act 1925, for the benefit of the covenant to pass at common law, written notice of the assignment should be given to the covenantor, ie, the party with the burden.

(ii) Conditions from P&A Swift Investment v Combined English Stores (1989)

4.12   The conditions from *P&A Swift* are that:

  (i)   Covenant must touch and concern the land;

  (ii) The parties must intend the benefit to pass;

  (iii) Successor in title to covenantee must hold a legal estate; AND,

  (iv) Original covenantee must have held a legal estate.

4.13   A covenant will **touch and concern the land** if it is for the benefit of the dominant land, affecting its **nature**, **quality**, **mode of use, or value**. Thus, anything expressed to be personal is not likely to satisfy this condition. For the parties to **intend the benefit to pass** they could use **express words**, or they could be implied **s78, Law of Property Act 1925**, which deems a covenant to be made with the covenantee and those who obtain the land from him, that is, his successors in title.

4.14   The requirement that the **successor in title to covenantee must hold a legal estate** is almost self-explanatory. The legal estates in land are those listed in **s1(1), Law of Property Act 1925**. The benefit will not pass where the covenantee has only an equitable interest in the dominant land. The final condition, namely that the **original covenantee must have held a legal estate**, is also straightforward. Note, the legal estate held does not have to be the same one (**Smith and Snipes Hall Farm Ltd v River Douglas Catchment Board (1949)**).

(iii) Contract (Rights of Third Parties) Act 1999

4.15   The 1999 Act requires a term in the agreement to give a third party some right of action, or to confer a benefit upon them. This is of limited significance.

(iv) s56, Law of Property Act 1925

4.16   This provision states that an individual may benefit from a covenant, even though not named in the conveyance.

Common Law (Burden)

Will the burden of a covenant pass to a new owner of the servient land at common law?

4.17   The general rule is that the **burden of a covenant will NOT pass at common law (Austerberry v Oldham Corporation (1885)(CA); Rhone v Stephens (1994)(HL)).** The original covenantor remains liable (**s79, Law of Property Act 1925**), but only for damages (**Tophams Ltd v Earl of Sefton (1967)**). However, there are some useful exceptions which you should know: (i) the 'chain of indemnity' covenants; (ii) the rule in *Halsall v Brizell*.

(i) 'chain of indemnity' covenants

4.18   One way of getting around the problem of enforceability at common law is that each time the burdened land is sold, an indemnity covenant could be obtained from the buyer for the benefit of the seller. This indemnity has the effect that if the original covenantor is sued for the buyer's breach of covenant, the buyer agrees to indemnify the seller, ie, pay the seller's damages. This can happen down the chain of buyers of the burdened land.

4.19 A chain of indemnity covenants would look like this diagram:

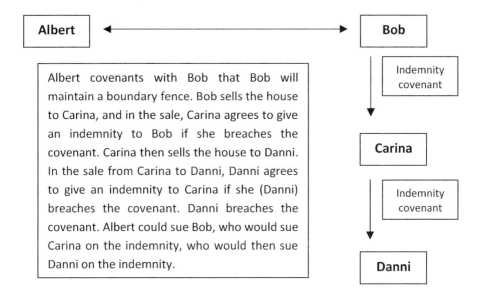

Albert covenants with Bob that Bob will maintain a boundary fence. Bob sells the house to Carina, and in the sale, Carina agrees to give an indemnity to Bob if she breaches the covenant. Carina then sells the house to Danni. In the sale from Carina to Danni, Danni agrees to give an indemnity to Carina if she (Danni) breaches the covenant. Danni breaches the covenant. Albert could sue Bob, who would sue Carina on the indemnity, who would then sue Danni on the indemnity.

4.20 Here, a positive covenant – a maintenance covenant – is agreed between Albert and Bob. Albert has the benefit and Bob has the burden, because he is likely have to spend money to maintain the boundary fence. This covenant is not enforceable in equity as it is positive. Equity will only enforce restrictive (negative) covenants. Therefore, Albert has to look at the common law exceptions. Fortunately, in this situation, an indemnity covenant has been given to each seller by the buyer. One was given from Carina to Bob, and another from Danni to Carina following each sale. This is important because Bob, as the original covenantor, remains liable as a matter of contract law, even though the estate has been sold on. So, Albert can sue Bob for damages for breach of covenant, even though it was breached by Danni. However, because of the first indemnity covenant, Bob will get his losses paid by Carina on the indemnity. What can Carina do? Well, she can rely on the indemnity covenant she obtained when she sold the land to have her losses covered by Danni.

4.21 Here, a chain of indemnities linking Bob to Carina and

Carina to Danni is created meaning that if Bob is sued for damages, Danni may ultimately be required to pay. Of course, it is only money. It does not get the fence fixed, but Danni might be of the view that to avoid future claims on the indemnity she agreed, it is simply worth paying to maintain the fence as the covenant requires.

4.22 Hopefully you can see the problem with the chain of indemnity covenants, that is, an indemnity must be obtained each time the burdened land is sold so that a 'chain' of indemnity covenants is created. Problematically, if on one sale the indemnity covenant is forgotten, the chain is broken; **the chain is only as strong as its weakest link**. The chain can also be broken by insolvency or unavailability of the party which agreed it.

4.23 Even where the chain is complete, enforcement is indirect and means that damages are passed down the 'chain'. The remedy the covenantee would usually want, eg, specific performance or an injunction, is not available to them.

4.24 It may be that a Restriction on the Proprietorship Register (s40, LRA 2002) could be entered to prevent sale of the burdened land *unless* the buyer agrees to enter into a direct arrangement where they promise to perform the burden of a positive covenant.

(ii) the rule in Halsall v Brizell

4.25 This is sometimes known as the rule of **mutual benefit and burden**. One party cannot deny they are subject to a burden if they also enjoy a benefit. A common example would be an obligation for one party to make a financial contribution to the maintenance of an access road which they use to access their land; they have the benefit of use of the road, so they should pay towards its maintenance. The rule has its origins in **Halsall v Brizell (1957)**, but has developed since that decision.

4.26 The modern expression of the conditions for the 'rule in Halsall v Brizell' come from **Davies v Jones (2009)(CA)**:

(1) The benefit and burden must be conferred in the same

transaction;

(2) The benefit and the burden must be linked in some way, as in the example provided in para 4.25, above. Whether this link is satisfied will often be a question of construction of the documents conferring the benefit and imposing the burden (**Wilkinson v Kerdene (2013)(CA)**);

(3) The individual subject to the burden must have the freedom to reject it, and thereby not be able to enjoy the benefit (**Thamesmead Town Ltd v Allotey (1998)**).

Equity (Burden)

Will the burden of a covenant pass to a new owner of the servient land in equity?

4.27   We will now consider the rules in equity, but we will start with the burden. The reason for this is that if the burden does not pass, there is no reason to consider the benefit in equity.

4.28   For the burden of a covenant to pass in equity, the following conditions must be satisfied:

(i)   The covenant must be negative in substance;

(ii) The covenant must accommodate the dominant tenement;

(iii) The original parties must have intended that the burden should bind successors;

(iv) The person against whom the covenant is being enforced must have notice of it.

(i)   The covenant must be negative in substance

4.29   The covenant must be negative in substance, even if the language sounds positive. Therefore, a covenant to maintain land as an open space, free of buildings, is negative in substance because it limits the erection of buildings, even though the language *sounds* positive (**Tulk v Moxhay (1848)**). Other examples include *to use premises for only business purposes*, or *retain the bungalow as only a single-storey dwelling*. The reason for this restriction is that equity will not require someone to carry out an act which involves spending money – putting their hand in their pocket (**Haywood v Brunswick Building Society (1881)**).

4.30   A covenant which is mixed, ie, partly positive and partly negative, may be severed and the negative part upheld (**Shepherd Homes Ltd v Sandham (No 2) (1971)**).

(ii)   The covenant must accommodate the dominant tenement

4.31   The covenant must be for the benefit of the land, not merely of benefit to the owner. Here, reliance is placed on **P & A Swift Investments v Combined English Stores (1989)** and whether the covenant touches and concerns the land, meaning the covenant affects the nature, quality, mode of use, or value, of the land. Allied to this is the notion that there must be a relationship of dominant and servient land (**London CC v Allen (1914)**).

(iii)   The original parties must have intended that the burden should bind successors

4.32   The original parties could have intended the burden should bind either by the use of **express wording in the original conveyance**, or place reliance on the *implied intention* under s79, Law of Property Act 1925. However, the statutory provision may not be relied upon where a contrary intention is expressed (**Morrells of Oxford Ltd v Oxford United FC (2000)**).

(iv)   The person against whom the covenant is being enforced must have notice of it

4.33   Whether the correct notice provisions apply depends on whether title to the land is unregistered or registered.

4.34   Where **title is unregistered**, they should be protected by a class D(ii) land charge and, where registered in this way, this constitutes notice (s198, LPA 1925). If it is not registered, a purchaser of the legal estate for money or money's worth is not bound (s4(6), Land Charges Act 1972). For covenants agreed before 1st January 1926, the doctrine of notice continues to apply.

4.35 Where **title is registered**, a **Notice** should be entered on the **Charges Register** of the burdened land (s32, LRA 2002). If not registered, the purchaser of the legal estate is not bound (s29, LRA 2002). However, the covenant will be effective against a non-purchaser even where the covenant is not registered (s28, LRA 2002). This means that if it is not registered, but the new owner *inherited* the estate following the death of the previous owner, the new owner will still be bound. The reason for this is that the new owner did not pay for the estate, and by getting something for nothing, they are better off than they were anyway!

Equity (Benefit)

Will the benefit of a covenant pass to a new owner of the dominant land in equity?

4.36 The answer to this question is 'Yes', provided the following are satisfied:

(i)   The covenant touches and concerns the land; AND,

(ii) The covenant has been either (a) Annexed to the land; (b) Assigned to the covenantee's successor; or, (c) there is a building scheme in place.

(i)   The covenant touches and concerns the land

4.37 Whether a covenant is for the benefit of the land will be determined, once again, by **P & A Swift Investments v Combined English Stores (1989)** and asking whether the covenant affects the **nature**, **quality**, **mode of use**, **or value**, of the land.

(ii)(a) Annexation

4.38 Annexation means 'attaching' the benefit of the covenant to the land. This can be done by express words or by the statutory wording in **s78, LPA 1925**, but while this provision implies words into all restrictive land covenants, the benefited land must be sufficiently clearly identified (**Bath Rugby Ltd v Greenwood and others (2021)**).

(ii)(b) Assignment

4.39 This is the process of transferring the benefit to the new covenantee every time the dominant land is sold. Note: The benefit must be assigned each time (**Miles v Easter (1933)**).

(iii)(c) Building Scheme

4.40 The final method is by a building scheme, essentially a housing estate, where covenants are made for the benefit of each and every landowner on the estate. The criteria for this were set down in **Elliston v Reacher (1908)**. They are:

(i) All purchasers acquire their property from the same (common) seller;

(ii) Before sale, the seller has divided the estate into plots;

(iii) Any restrictive covenants were intended by the seller to continue to benefit the plots;

(iv) Each buyer purchases a plot understanding that the covenants benefit all the other plots in the scheme.

4.41 The criteria under 'building schemes' are difficult to meet.

Reform

4.42   As can be seen, the law in this area is a complex of rules and conditions which must be satisfied. With this in mind, there has been an agenda for reform for a number of years. In 2011, the Law Commission published a report, 'Easements, Covenants and Profits à Prendre' (Law Com No327), with a Bill annexed for reform of the law.

4.43   The principal reforms recommended to the law on covenants involve simplification of the law of restrictive covenants, making life easier for buyers of land, and allowing for the **benefit and burden of positive obligations** to be enforced by, and against, owners of the dominant and servient land. This would replace the covenant with a generic '**land obligation**' label.

CHAPTER 5
EASEMENTS AND PROFITS

Introduction

5.01   An easement is a property right enjoyed against another's land. Most easements are **positive**, ie, allowing the holder of the easement to do something on the neighbour's land, eg, an easement of way across your neighbour's land – that's the classic easement. However, easements might also be **negative**, which effectively restricts your neighbour's use of their land. A good example would be an easement of light which restricts your neighbour from building on their land in any way which might restrict the light to your land. With negative easements there is, of course, an overlap with restrictive covenants (see chapter four), which is why the law is careful not to recognise too many negative easements (**Phipps v Pears (1964)**).

5.02   To determine whether a right which is claimed is a valid easement: First, it must have the **characteristics of an easement**; secondly, it must have been **acquired as an easement**; thirdly, it must have been **protected in the correct way**. This chapter will follow this order.

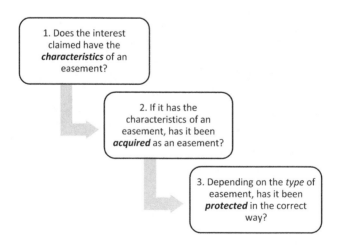

1. Does the interest claimed have the *characteristics* of an easement?

2. If it has the characteristics of an easement, has it been *acquired* as an easement?

3. Depending on the *type* of easement, has it been *protected* in the correct way?

Characteristics of Easements

5.03   For an interest claimed to have the characteristics of an easement, it needs to satisfy the criteria from **Re Ellenbrough Park (1956)**, confirmed by the recent Supreme Court case of **Regency Villas Ltd v Diamond Resorts Ltd (2018)**. They are:

(i)   There must be a dominant and a servient tenement;

(ii)   The right must accommodate the dominant tenement;

(iii) The dominant and servient tenements must be owned or occupied by different people;

(iv)   The interest must lie in grant.

5.04   While these are the principal criteria, there are other factors which also need to be considered: (v) No expenditure by servient tenement; (vi) Is it recreational?; (vii) May not be exclusive possession.

(i)   There must be a dominant and a servient tenement

5.05   For every right which purports to be an easement, there must be a dominant tenement to enjoy the right, and a servient tenement over which the right is exercised. 'Tenement' simply means 'land' in this context; so, there must be dominant and servient land.

5.06   The dominant and servient tenements must be identifiable at the time of the creation of the claimed easement (**London & Blenheim Estates ltd v Ladbroke Retail Parks Ltd (1994)**).

5.07   It is often said that an easement cannot exist 'in gross', ie, separate from dominant land which can enjoy it.

5.08   This requirement is easily satisfied in most cases.

(ii)   The right must accommodate the dominant tenement

5.09   The right must be for the benefit of the dominant tenement. This has been interpreted to mean more than merely increasing the economic value of the land, though that will be a key issue in some cases, but that accommodating the dominant tenement means that the supposed easement should relate to the *normal enjoyment of the land* (**Regency Villas Ltd v Diamond Resorts Ltd (2018)** echoing the language of **Re Ellenborough Park (1956)**).

5.10   In *Regency Villas*, Lord Briggs JSC, provided a good example of what was meant by this *distinction*. He provides that the right of a house in Kennington, south London, near to the Oval cricket ground, to have free access to the cricket ground on match days might be valuable, especially to a cricket fan, but have little to do with the normal use of the property as a home. Thus, though an increase in value might be seen as accommodating the dominant tenement, it is the easement as it relates to the normal enjoyment of the land which is the key issue to determine.

5.11   A further element of this criterion is that there must be sufficient proximity between the dominant and servient tenements. They do not *literally* have to be next to one another (**Pugh v Savage (1970)**), so long as the servient tenement is sufficiently close to the dominant tenement to provide a practical benefit to it. Though they do not need to share a boundary fence, it is the case that there cannot be an easement over land in Northumberland for the benefit of land in Kent (**Bailey v Stephens (1862)**).

5.12   For an easement to accommodate the dominant tenement, it must also be more than a mere personal advantage to the person claiming the right. Easements are, after all, property rights, so they should benefit the land, not merely the person claiming it! A good example of this is the case of **Hill v Tupper (1863)** where a canal company leased land adjoining a canal to Hill giving him the exclusive right to let out pleasure boats on the canal. Tupper, an inn-keeper who owned premises abutting the canal, began to let his own boats on the canal. Hill sued Tupper for interference with his alleged easement. The court held that Hill's right was personal, a licence, and that Tupper's action was not an interference with a property right. Hill did not have an easement, so could not sue Tupper for interference with it.

5.13 By contrast, in **Moody v Steggles (1879)**, a pub-owner fixed signs on a neighbouring house directing passers-by to his pub which was set-back from the main high street. This was held to be an easement since it conferred the right on the land, as it was connected to the use of the land as a pub, and not on the person who was, from time-to-time, the landlord of the pub. This thread of reasoning can be found in the case of **P&S Platt v Crouch (2003)**.

5.14 I would like to flag one more thing before moving on. Some textbooks add a further element to this characteristic and that is that an easement cannot be *purely recreational* as that has not been seen *traditionally* as accommodating the dominant tenement. I don't suppose that it matters a great deal, but I deal with this point later. However, what I will say is that the important element is that you understand the current position, namely that recreational easements can be for the benefit of the land. See, later, paras 5.25 – 5.26.

(iii) The dominant and servient tenements must be owned or occupied by different people

5.15 Since an easement is a right one enjoys over another's land, it stands to reason that the lands in question must be owned or occupied by different persons. I cannot enjoy an easement against myself (**Roe v Siddons (1889)**). The stipulation that the land be owned *or occupied* means that landlord and tenant relationships do not infringe the characteristic. For example, Bob owns Whiteacre and Greenacre; they are adjoining properties. Bob leases Greenacre to Clara. Some while later, Bob grants Clara an easement across Whiteacre so Clara can store items in a shed on Whiteacre. This could be a valid easement, even though Bob is the freehold owner of both Whiteacre and Greenacre, but importantly, Clara is the leaseholder of Greenacre.

(iv) The interest must lie in grant

5.16 The easement must be a right which is capable of being granted by a grantor (party giving the easement) to a grantee (party receiving the easement). This simplistic statement has more to it. Time for a table of the elements of this characteristic:

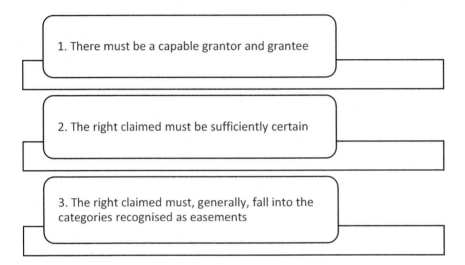

1. There must be a capable grantor and grantee

2. The right claimed must be sufficiently certain

3. The right claimed must, generally, fall into the categories recognised as easements

5.17 Let's break each of these down. First, there must be a **capable grantor and grantee**, meaning the parties are of full age and sound mind, and that the grantor is in possession of an estate in the servient tenement, and that the grantee is in possession of an estate in the dominant tenement.

5.18 Secondly, the right must be sufficiently certain. When you are a legal professional and a client tells you that they have agreed an easement with their neighbour and that they would like you to draft it, that is an onerous task. You have to put the client's words into legal language which can be understood by others and, if necessary, enforced. Thus, the thing they ask for cannot be too vague and uncertain. If it's an easement of way, then that it straightforward enough, but what if it is an easement of a view? How would it be possible to draft that? Well, in all likelihood it would be impossible to describe a view accurately in writing

(**William Aldred's Case (1610)**), or a right to privacy (**Browne v Fowler (1911)**). Therefore, whatever is claimed must be capable of a sufficient level of certainty.

5.19   Thirdly, the right claimed must, generally speaking, fall into the category of easements recognised as such. This almost speaks for itself. If the supposed easement being claimed is one which has been judicially-recognised before, then it should pass that element. Does this mean that there will be no new easements? Of course not, but it does mean that if you are asking for a supposed easement, you have a better chance if it has already happened.

5.20   A good modern example of this, and the reluctance of courts to recognise new easements, comes from **Hunter v Canary Wharf Limited (1997)**. During the building of the Canary Wharf complex in the former docklands of east London, residents in the local area became aware that the high-rise office blocks being built began to interfere with the television signal to their property. The residents claimed that they had an easement of receipt of a television signal. The House of Lords disagreed and said that there was no such easement.

5.21   In these paragraphs we have discussed the key elements of the characteristics of an easement. However, there are other elements which I flagged to you in para 5.04 and we turn to consider those now.

(v) No expenditure by servient tenement

5.22   Generally, the servient owner should not be required to spend money (**Duke of Westminster v Guild (1985)**). The role of the servient owner is passive in that they merely allow the dominant owner to exercise their right without interference. Therefore, an interest claimed which requires the servient owner to undertake positive acts is not, generally, characteristic of an easement.

5.23   There are, however, exceptions. For example, maintenance of a boundary fence has been upheld as a valid easement, even though it would involve the servient owner spending money (**Crow v Wood (1971)**). In the recent case of **Churston Golf Club Ltd v Haddock (2019)**, the CA declined to interpret what was clearly a positive covenant as an easement of fencing because the wording of the provision did not support that interpretation. This reversed the High Court decision in the case. Thus, it seems that for an easement of fencing to be found, the language must be clear that what it is creating is an easement of fencing.

5.24 In **Regency Villas Ltd v Diamond Resorts Ltd (2018)**, the SC held that owners of timeshare properties could benefit from valid easements to use sporting facilities and gardens surrounding the property. This was so notwithstanding running costs and operational responsibilities imposed on the servient owner by the easement.

(vi) Is it recreational?

5.25 Historically, the law was troubled by recreational easements because they were not typical of the sort of easements which might be valid. Easements should not, it was thought, be about personal recreational enjoyment. This shifted slightly with the case of **Re Ellenborough Park (1956)**, where the court held that use of a formal garden connected with normal enjoyment of land could amount to an easement. However, the recent case of **Regency Villas Ltd v Diamond Resorts Ltd (2018)** seems to have broadened the law to such a degree that recreational easements are a recognised part of the law.

5.26 In *Regency Villas*, owners of timeshare properties in Kent were provided with a wide-range of recreational facilities as part of the timeshare arrangement. These included a swimming pool, squash courts, an 18-hole golf course, extensive grounds, and indoor facilities including a restaurant, bar, and gym. However, these facilities were either gradually removed or not maintained and the timeshare owners claimed an interference with property rights as easements. The Supreme Court upheld the claims of the timeshare owners. The rights, the Supreme Court held, though in the nature of recreational rights, were capable of accommodating the dominant tenement. The facilities were of *service, utility and benefit* to the timeshare owners and would benefit any owner, from time-to-time of the timeshare properties.

(vii) May not be exclusive possession

5.27   An easement should not mean that the servient owner is denied the use of their land. In other words, the easement should not allow the dominant owner effective occupation of the servient land. However, some easements create problems for this objection and they are easements of storage (**Wright v Macadam (1949)**) and easements of parking (**Batchelor v Marlow (2003)**).

5.28   The courts have considered whether the use by the dominant owner amounts to exclusive possession in the context of parking in two cases in the last 20-odd years. In **Batchelor v Marlow (2003)**, the CA set down the **'degree' test** asking whether the right granted would leave the servient owner with any **reasonable use of their land**. *Would the servient owner be left with any reasonable use of their land?* If it could not be shown that the servient owner retained some reasonable use, then there could be no easement. In *Batchelor*, the dominant owner claimed a right to park six cars on the servient land between 830am and 6pm. The court said this removed any *reasonable use* from the servient owner, therefore there was no easement.

5.29   At this point, it is worth mentioning the Scottish appeal to the House of Lords in **Moncrieff v Jamieson (2008)** on the parking easement issue. There, a **'possession and control' test** was preferred. Does the servient owner retain possession and control of their land where there is reasonable use of the easement by the dominant owner? If so, then there will be an easement.

5.30   Naturally, the court is seeking to strike a balance between allowing valid easements, without undermining the ownership of the servient owner. As to which test should be followed, technically, the test from *Batchelor* is binding, but the law on easements in England is substantially the same as its Scottish counterpart (servitudes), so *Moncrieff* could be easily applicable in England and Wales.

Positive and Negative Easements

5.31   As stated, easements can be positive or negative and they may develop as society and circumstances develop. The categories of easements are not closed (**Dyce v Lady Hay (1852)**). While the courts have been willing to recognise new, novel, positive easements, eg, to use land to move aircraft (**Dowty Boulton Paul Ltd v Wolverhampton Corporation (No 2) (1976)**), and to hang washing (**Drewell v Towler (1832)**), recognising new negative easements is something more of a challenge (**Phipps v Pears (1964)**).

Acquisition of Easements

5.32   Once a right claimed has the characteristics of an easement, the next stage is to determine whether the interest has been **acquired as an easement**. An easement might be acquired in a number of ways:

(i)   Express grant or reservation;

(ii)   Implied grant or reservation;

   (a) Common intention;

   (b) Necessity;

(iii) Rule in Wheeldon v Burrows (Grant only);

(iv)   Section 62, Law of Property Act 1925 (Grant only);

(v)   Prescription.

5.33   Before considering these in detail, it is first necessary to make clear the **terminology** of **grant** and **reservation**.

5.34   To **grant is to give a right**, while to **reserve is to keep a right**. For example, Andy owns Blackacre and Greenacre. They are adjoining properties. Andy leased Blackacre to Carey. In the lease, Andy gave (granted) Carey the right to cross over Greenacre so Carey could access a garage. Here, Andy **granted the easement** to Carey. Andy's land is the servient land, and Carey's land the dominant land.

5.35 Alternatively, if, in the same scenario, where Andy leased Blackacre to Carey, Andy needed access over Blackacre to get to the main road, Andy would retain (reserve) a right to cross Blackacre from Greenacre to get to the main road. Here, Andy **reserves an easement of way** to cross Blackacre. Andy's land is the dominant land, and Carey's land is the servient land.

(i)   Express grant or reservation

5.36   An expressly granted or reserved easement is one which has been deliberately created by an individual. It is expressed in the document which creates the transfer. In paragraph 5.34, above, there is an example of an express grant. In paragraph 5.35, above, there is an example of an express reservation.

(ii)   Implied grant or reservation

5.37   Where the parties haven't considered the easement, one may be *implied* **into the document creating the transfer**. Easements can be implied in a number of different ways, by **grant or reservation**. There are four ways easements can be implied: (i) **common intention** and (ii) **necessity**, (iii), the **rule in Wheeldon v Burrows**, (iv) **section 62, Law of Property Act 1925**, and (v) **prescription**. However, and this is important, only (i) and (ii) can be implied by grant or reservation, whereas (iii), (iv), and (v) **OPERATE IN GRANT** *only*.

*(i)   Implied grant or reservation – **Common intention***

5.38   Implied easements by common intention **give effect to the common intention of the parties** by reference to the manner or purposes for which the land was granted to be used (**Pwllback Colliery Co Ltd v Woodman (1915)**). The more modern approach is expressed in the case of **Stafford v Lee (1992)**. In the case of *Stafford*, the claimant (Stafford) obtained planning permission on woodland in order to build a house on the land. The only access for construction traffic was across the defendant's (Lee's) land, who contended that the access was only for purposes connected to the woodland and not for construction works. The claimant sought a declaration from the court that such traffic had access across the defendant's land, but also that there would be future access for all purposes connected with the land. In granting the declaration, the court held that it was the common intention of the parties that Stafford's land should enjoy an easement over Lee's land.

5.39 The court found for the claimant, Stafford, and in doing so clarified the elements crucial for an easement to be implied by common intention. First, there **should be evidence of common (agreed) intention between the parties of some *definite and particular purpose or user*** and, secondly, that the **easement was *necessary to give effect to that common stated purpose or user***. The two-stage approach from *Stafford* was affirmed by the Court of Appeal in **Donovan v Rana (2014)**.

(ii) Implied grant or reservation – **Necessity**

5.40 Implied easements by necessity are used where, without the easement, the land would not be possible to use. The most common example is that of land which, without the easement, would otherwise be landlocked, that is, *it could not be accessed by land*. This method of acquisition is very strictly applied, so even if a less convenient means of access to land is available, an easement of necessity will not be implied. For example, in **Manjang v Drammeh (1990)** the land in dispute was bordered on three sides by land belonging to other individuals, but on its fourth side was the River Gambia, a publicly navigable river. The claimant, arguing an implied easement of necessity, sought access by land over neighbouring land. The court refused the claim on the basis that as the owner wasn't technically locked out of his land because of the River Gambia giving him access by water, he should use that means of access.

5.41   This may be considered a somewhat harsh decision, but it illustrates three things. First, an easement by necessity will only be permitted in the narrowest range of cases, that is, where there is no meaningful access by land or water. Secondly, it illustrates the importance of the buyer ensuring that they have all the rights in place which they believe will be need in order to use the land acquired. Thirdly, and finally, there is nothing to prevent the landowner from purchasing an easement from a neighbouring landowner.

5.42   In all, *Manjang* sends a clear message to buyers: An easement of necessity will only be granted where the land would be impossible to use without the easement, not because the landowner merely wants the easement because the easement would provide a *more convenient* means of access to the land.

5.43   An interesting comment on the strictness of necessity can be seen in the first instance decision of **Sweet v Sommer (2004)**. In this case, the claimants did not have access by vehicle to their land, but access on foot along what happened to be a public footpath, so contended that it was *effectively* landlocked.

5.44   The first instance judge said, in relation to cases with access by some means, but not by vehicle, it cannot be reasoned that just because one judge in one case says that a house in a particular location is usable in the ordinary sense of the word without being accessible by vehicles, that the same is true of all houses everywhere. Instead, courts should look at the circumstances and consider whether it is so obvious from the nature of the particular house and the circumstances that **access by vehicle was regarded as necessary to its use** and that access by foot, or equally less convenient means, would mean that the land is not effectively useable without an easement of necessity by vehicular access. So, it would seem that the courts *may* be willing to take a more flexible approach to such easements.

(iii)   ***Rule in Wheeldon v Burrows (Grant only)***

5.45 This method of acquisition **operates in grant *only***. This is one area of land law where the rule can be explained by a diagram. Well, in this case, two diagrams, and think of them as before and after:

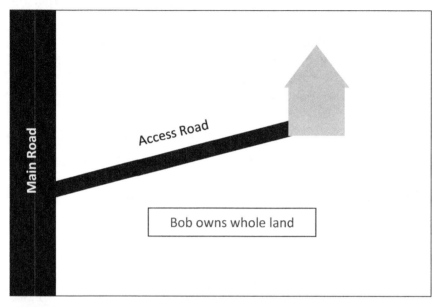

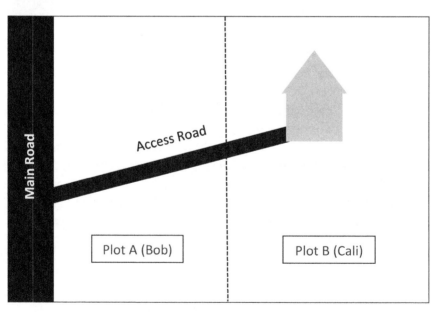

5.46   Now, take a good look at those diagrams. In the first, Bob owns the whole of the land. To get to his (grey and uninspiring) house, Bob turns off the main road which is a public highway, and drives along his own private access road, that is, his drive. Bob does not need easements because he is accessing his own land over his own drive. Now, time marches on and Bob is running out of money. So, he has an idea! He decides to divide his land into plots, 'Plot A' and 'Plot B'. He keeps 'Plot A' for himself and sells 'Plot B', which has the house on it, to Cali. Unfortunately, Bob's lawyer is a bit dim and forgets to grant Cali an easement over 'Plot A' so that she can get to her new home on 'Plot B'. This is a problem for Cali as she cannot get to the (grey and uninspiring) house. Luckily, help is on hand in the form of the **rule in Wheeldon v Burrows**.

5.47   The rule in Wheeldon v Burrows, also known as the rule of quasi-easements, allows Cali to claim an easement is implied into the grant (the conveyance) of 'Plot B' to her on the basis that *effectively*, when Bob owned the whole of the land (before he split it in two) he enjoyed a quasi-easement, that is, a right which is *like an easement*, over the first part of the 'Access Road'. Therefore, when he split the land and sold 'Plot B' to Cali, that quasi-easement passed as a full easement to Cali as current owner of 'Plot B'. Remember, Bob did not need an easement *initially* because he owned the whole of the land and could not have an *easement against himself*. However, had the land been split at the time he owned 'Plot B' and someone else had occupied 'Plot A', he would have used the 'Access Road' as an easement to access 'Plot B'.

5.48   There are requirements to meet from **Wheeldon v Burrows (1879)** in order to pass a full easement to Cali. The requirements of **Wheeldon v Burrows** are that:

(a)   The use of the quasi-easement was continuous and apparent;

(b)   It was necessary for the reasonable enjoyment of the land granted; and,

(c)   It was used by the grantor for the benefit of the land granted.

5.49   Let's consider each of these elements in a little more detail.

(a)   The use of the quasi-easement was continuous and apparent

5.50   An easement is **continuous** if it is the right to do something which is **continuous in nature**. An **apparent** easement is one which is **obvious from examination of the land** by a person ordinarily conversant with the subject. For example, drains and paths might be continuous and apparent (**Ward v Kirkland (1967)**), as well as a right to light through a defined window (**Phillips v Low (1892)**), a right of way defined by tarmacked roadway (**Millman v Ellis (1996)**; **Hillman v Rogers (1998)**), and an underground drain into which water runs from the eaves of a house (**Watts v Kelson (1870)**; **McAdams Homes Ltd v Robinson (2004)**).

(b)   It was necessary for the reasonable enjoyment of the land granted

5.51   There is some debate in this area over the words **necessary** and **reasonable** and how they relate to **continuous and apparent**. It would seem, following recent cases, that **continuous and apparent** does not stand alone but should be read alongside this requirement (**Alford v Hannaford (2011)(CA)**; **Wood v Waddington (2015)(CA)**). In terms of *reasonably necessary*, it appears that the emphasis rests on the word **reasonable (Wheeler v JJ Saunders (1996)(CA))**.

(c)   It was used by the grantor for the benefit of the land granted

5.52   This is fairly self-explanatory in that the quasi-easement must be in use by the grantor at the date of the transfer. Interestingly, in **Kent v Kavanagh (2007)(CA)**, a claim to an easement was rejected because the quasi-easement was in use by a tenant at the time of the transfer.

5.53   The rule in Wheeldon v Burrows can be excluded by express words in the conveyance. It would also appear that a conveyance which also includes a fencing covenant designed to cut-off access may defeat the operation of the rule in *Wheeldon v Burrows* as indicated in **Browning v Jack (2021)**, a decision of the Lands Tribunal.

(iv) *Section 62, Law of Property Act 1925 (Grant only)*

5.54   Section 62, LPA 1925 is a word-saving provision used by conveyancers and ensures that conveyances (land transfers) include all those things one might expect to be included, particularly for our purposes, it includes rights, easements, etc. However, s62, LPA 1925 has been held to have the curious effect of elevating a mere permission to an easement (**Wright v Macadam (1949)**; **Hair v Gillman (2000)**).

5.55   The section operates on the following conditions:

    (i)   There must be a conveyance of a legal lease, freehold, or mortgage by deed;

    (ii)   There must be evidence of prior use;

    (iii)   No contrary intention expressed (**s62(4), LPA 1925**); and,

    (iv)   Right claimed must be capable of being an easement, so the *Ellenbrough Park* criteria must be satisfied.

5.56   Previously, it was thought that prior diversity of ownership or occupation was needed (**Sovmots Investments Ltd v Secretary of State for the Environment (1979)**). This means that before the transfer, the plots of land should have been owned or occupied by different people. However, this this no longer seems to be the case (**P & S Platt Ltd v Crouch (2004)(CA)**, confirmed in **Wood v Waddington (2015)(CA)**).

5.57   The decisions of *P & S Platt Ltd v Crouch* and *Wood v*

Waddington, by doing away with the requirement of prior diversity of occupation, does bring into question the continuing significance of the rule in *Wheeldon v Burrows*. The reason for this is that by dropping the prior diversity requirement for section 62, the statutory provision is significantly broadened in its operation. That said, the rule in *Wheeldon v Burrows* is not dead yet and was applied in the recent Tribunal decision of **Taurusbuild Ltd v McQue (2019)**, where it passed a quasi-easement to a mortgagee in possession, which was then subsequently passed to a purchaser of the repossessed property, the McQues, by s62, LPA 1925. So, this case demonstrates the two methods can work alongside one another.

(v)   Prescription

5.58   The final method of acquiring an easement is by **prescription**, or **long use**. This method has it that so long as it can be shown that an easement has been in use for some time, the easement might operate by this method.

5.59   There are three ways of establishing an easement by long use:

(i)   Common Law;

(ii)   Doctrine of Lost Modern Grant;

(iii) Prescription Act 1832.

(i)   Common Law

5.60   At common law, it is presumed the grant of easement was made before 1189 (the date of legal memory), unless it can be shown not to have existed at the time, or could not have existed at some point since that time.

5.61   To bring the claim, it must be shown that the use was **without force**, **without secrecy**, and **without permission**, but proving common law prescription is difficult.

(ii) Doctrine of Lost Modern Grant

5.62 The doctrine of lost modern grant supplements the common law position making a presumption that the grant was made in the past but has been lost, hence, *lost modern grant*. A period of 20 years use must be shown, but it does not have to have immediately preceded the claim. Occasional use will suffice for the purposes of lost modern grant, even by a small number of visitors over a period of time (**Hughes v Incumbent of the benefice of Frampton-on-Severn, Arlingham, Saul, Fretherne and Framilode (2021)**).

(iii) Prescription Act 1832

5.63 Under the Prescription Act 1832, there are two designated periods of time: 20 years and 40 years. If a right has been established for **40 years**, it is deemed **absolute and indefeasible**. If the right is by the 20 year period, it cannot be defeated merely by showing that it cannot have existed at some point since 1189.

5.64 The claim must be as of right, and must be for the period immediately preceding the claim, unlike with the doctrine of lost modern grant.

5.65 Where an **easement of light** is concerned, the right is deemed **absolute and indefeasible** where the right has been enjoyed for **20 years without interruption**, unless enjoyed by agreement or consent.

Terminating an Easement

5.66 Yes, easements can come to an end, and may do so in a number of ways. First, an easement can come to an end when the **dominant and servient land come into single ownership**. Secondly, the servient land can be released from the burden of an easement by **deed or abandonment**. Thirdly, an easement can be extinguished by **estoppel**. Fourthly, that it has become **obsolete**. Fifthly, and finally, an easement can be extinguished by

excessive use. If an easement was first designated for a particular purpose, but that the character of the neighbourhood has changed so that it is being used more frequently or with heavier vehicles, the easement could be extinguished by excessive use. The reason for this is that the current use is a greater burden to the servient land than was originally agreed under the initial grant of the easement.

Formalities and Protection of Easements

5.67   As with everything in land law, the scheme of protection of interests must be considered. Naturally, the answer will differ depending on whether title to the land is **registered** or **unregistered**. Additionally, it is also important to consider the formalities in the creation of easements. Fundamentally, an easement is a property interest in land, so it can be binding on a new owner of the servient land, but how?

Express Legal Easements

5.68   An express legal easement is an interest in land under s1(2)(a), LPA 1925, provided they are **granted for the equivalent of a freehold or leasehold estate**. It would need to be by deed (s52, LPA 1925; s1, LP(MP)A 1989) and once created, registered, in order to be **binding in registered title**.

5.69   Registration creates a little complexity, but not much. Effectively, both the benefit and the burden should be registered in the affected titles. The starting point is that expressly granted or reserved legal easements are registrable dispositions under s27(2)(d), LRA 2002. This means that if the interest is not registered, it will lose its status as a legal easement. So, the **benefit** should be protected in the registered title of the dominant owner, effectively meaning that they are the proprietor of a registered legal estate in the easement. The **burden** should be registered as a Notice on the Charges Register of the burdened title, that is, the servient owner's title. Once registered, it will bind a subsequent owner of the servient land, whether that person bought the land, inherited the land under a will, or was given it by the previous owner.

5.70 Where title to the land is unregistered, as a legal interest, the easement **would bind the whole world** without registration in any form.

Implied Legal Easements

5.71 An implied legal easement includes easements impliedly granted or reserved or easements acquired by prescription. In order for **implied legal easements** to be binding on a new owner of the land in **registered title, there is *nothing to do*!** Why? Well, implied legal easements override under sch 3, para 3, Land Registration Act 2002. In other words, they are binding without the need for registration.

5.72 That said, there are conditions which operate in respect of sch 3, para 3:

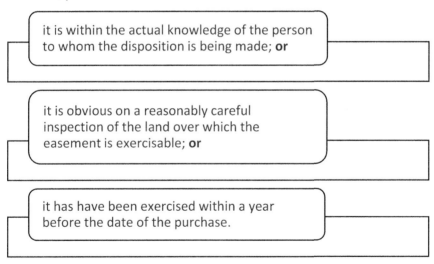

it is within the actual knowledge of the person to whom the disposition is being made; **or**

it is obvious on a reasonably careful inspection of the land over which the easement is exercisable; **or**

it has have been exercised within a year before the date of the purchase.

5.73 Where title is **unregistered**, as a legal interest, it **would bind the whole world** without registration of any form.

Equitable Easements

5.74   Where title is registered, all equitable easements are protected in the same way, namely as a **Notice on the Charges Register** (s32, LRA 2002) otherwise, a purchaser takes free of it (s29, LRA 2002). Interestingly, it has been said, albeit obiter, in the case of **Chaudhary v Yavuz (2013)**, that an equitable easement may be an interest which overrides under sch 3, para 2, LRA 2002. However, if this were to work, it would only operate in respect of certain easements which might be said to represent occupation easements, eg, storage easements.

5.75   Where **title** is **unregistered**, it would be protected as either a **D(iii) Land Charge**, otherwise the purchaser for value takes free of it (s4(6), Land Charges Act 1972).

5.76   Equitable easements created before 1st January 1926 are subject to the doctrine of notice.

Profits à prendre

5.77   A profit à prendre (or profit, for short) is the right to take something from another's land. A good example is the right to shoot or fish another's land. A profit may be granted by the landowner by deed, or it may be acquired by prescription at common law, or by the doctrine of lost modern grant. A profit may not, however, be found under prescription as set down in the Prescription Act 1832. A profit is capable of being registered with its own title under the Land Registration Act 2002.

CHAPTER 6
MORTGAGES

Introduction

6.01   A mortgage is an interest in land (s1(2)(c), LPA 1925) which is capable of being legal. That means it can be legal or equitable depending on how it is created. Technically, it is the grant, by the land owner, of an interest in land to another, usually a lender, as a security for the repayment of money borrowed by the borrower from the lender. So, in plain language, it is a sum of money advanced in return for security over a house.

6.02   Now, before we go any further, let's get the terminology straight. The **mortgagor is the borrower** and they are the party which grants the mortgage over their land (house) to the **mortgagee, who is the lender**. Students get these two terms mixed up all the time, so here is an easy way to remember. The **mOrtgagOr** is the **bOrrOwer**, and both words contain the letter 'O' twice. The **mortgagEE** is the **lEndEr**, and both words contain the letter 'E' twice. So, never get confused again!

Legal and Equitable Mortgages

6.03   As indicated at 6.01, a mortgage is an interest in land which is *capable of being legal*. This means that a mortgage can be legal or equitable. So, what makes it legal? A legal mortgage has to be created by deed (s52, LPA 1925), the requirements of which are that it must be in writing, signed by the grantor, witnessed, and delivered, which means it must be dated (s1, LP(MP)A 1989). This is the first stage. The second stage, to ensure that the mortgage is definitely legal, is that it must be registered (s27(2)(f), LRA 2002). Once both stages are complete, a valid legal mortgage is created.

6.04   An equitable mortgage is created in one of two ways. First, an equitable mortgage will be created where the interest which is mortgaged is equitable *only*. Secondly, an equitable mortgage would be created where an attempted legal mortgage is defective. A legal mortgage could be defective where the document used to create it did not satisfy the requirements for a valid deed. In such circumstances, the equitable mortgage would have to meet the requirements for a valid contract, that is, it must be in writing, contain all the terms of the agreement, and be signed by both parties (s2, LP(MP)A 1989).

Mortgagor's Protections: The Equity of Redemption

6.05   Over the years, certain protections have been developed to protect the mortgagor (borrower). These are known as the '**Equity of Redemption**' and the '**Equitable Right to Redeem**'.

6.06   The 'Equity of Redemption' means **all the mortgagor's rights without the obligations which the mortgagor owes to the mortgagee.**

6.07   On the other hand, the 'Equitable Right to Redeem' is the **right of the mortgagor to redeem the mortgage**, that is, to repay the loan, and take the property free of the mortgage. This right arises *after* the **common law date of redemption**. At common law, the borrower had to repay the mortgage on the legal date of redemption, ie, the legal date for repayment set down in the contract. Failure to repay on this fixed date entitled the lender to take the property. This was harsh, so that equity intervened to create the equitable right to redeem. This is the idea that so long as the borrower repaid the money as required, the lender could not claim the property; 'once a mortgage, always a mortgage' (Lord Parker in **Kreglinger v New Patagonia Meat and Cold Storage Company (1915)**). Over time, the equity of redemption developed into a series of rights so that there could be *no clogs or fetters* on the equitable right to redeem. In other words, there could be no restrictions on the right to redeem the property free of the mortgage.

6.08   So, what could be a clog or fetter on the equitable right to redeem? Well, attempts to postpone the date of redemption; attempts to give the mortgagee the option to purchase the mortgaged land; any attempt by the mortgagee to exploit the situation by taking perks from the mortgagor; or, any unconscionable terms. Let's look at each of these in a little more detail.

(i) postponed date of redemption

6.09 If the lender imposes a date of redemption so far into the future it makes the right to redeem illusory (an illusion), that is, not realistic, it will not be binding on the borrower. In **Fairclough v Swan Brewery Co Ltd (1912)**, a clause which postponed the date of redemption until six weeks before the lease expired was void, whereas in **Knightsbridge Estates Trust Ltd v Byrne (1939)**, postponement for 40 years from the date of the loan was upheld as the parties to the transaction were commercial parties.

6.10 The power to redeem a mortgage is contained in s91, LPA 1925.

(ii) option to purchase

6.10 When a mortgage is given, the lender cannot insist on an option to purchase the property (**Samuel v Jarrah Timber and Wood Paving Corporation Ltd (1904)**), unless it is granted after the mortgage is created so that it looks like a separate transaction (**Reeve v Lisle (1902)**).

(iii) collateral advantages

6.11 When a mortgage is given, the lender cannot also claim other things (perks) in addition to the right to repayment. To give these their technical name, they are *collateral advantages*. For example, in **Noakes & Co Ltd v Rice (1902)**, a tenant landlord of a pub was required to purchase certain alcohol only from the brewery lender, even after the mortgage was repaid. The court held the clause was void. By contrast, **Biggs v Hoddinott (1898)** upheld a similar arrangement since the requirement to buy alcohol from the brewery lender was limited to the mortgage period.

6.12 So, it would seem that the length of the commitment may provide the answer to whether the collateral advantage is enforceable, but not always. Sometimes, the relationship of the parties and the benefits of the transaction will influence the decision. For example, in **Kreglinger v New Patagonia Meat & Cold Storage Co Ltd (1914)**, the agreement continued *after* the mortgage term ended, but this was upheld as it was a proper commercial transaction which benefited both parties.

(iv) unconscionable terms

6.13 Unconscionable terms is a broad phrase including collateral advantages and excessive interest rates. Situations where the interest rate is excessive can void the mortgage (**Cityland and Property Holdings Ltd v Dabrah (1968)**). However, where the parties enter into a transaction with their eyes wide open, understanding the mortgage terms, possibly taking legal advice, the courts will not intervene, no matter how oppressive the term (**Multiservice Bookbinding Ltd v Marden (1978)**). This is because the courts would be allowing the mortgagor to escape from a bad bargain if they struck down the agreed rate of interest.

6.14 Unconscionable terms relating to the rate of interest charged on a mortgage are governed by the unfair relationships test in s140A, Consumer Credit Act 1974 (as amended).

6.15 Additionally, the Law of Property Act 1925 gives the borrower further statutory rights:

> Section 91 – gives the borrower a power to redeem the mortgage which can be enforced by the court;
>
> Section 99 – gives the borrower a power to lease the property for certain purposes and the power to accept surrenders of existing leases. This power may be modified by the terms of the mortgage;
>
> Section 98 – gives the borrower power to claim possession of the mortgaged property where the mortgagee does not claim possession;

Sections 91(1) and 91(2) – These provisions allow a borrower to apply to the court for an order for sale of the property which the court may decide to grant even if the mortgagee is opposed (**Palk v Mortgage Services Funding plc (1993)**). This right to apply is important where the borrower cannot pay instalments due on a mortgage causing the debt to mount up. A sale at this time can be advantageous, even if the house sells for less than the outstanding mortgage (negative equity), as it can prevent debts mounting up; this is what happened in *Palk*.

Enforcing a mortgage – the rights and remedies of the mortgagee

6.16   The lender enjoys a number of rights and remedies under a mortgage:

(i)   right to possession;

(ii) power of sale;

(iii) appointment of a receiver;

(iv) foreclosure;

(i) possession

6.17   A lender has the right to take possession of the mortgaged property (s95(4), LPA 1925) *before the ink is dry on the mortgage* (**Four Maids Ltd v Dudley Marshall (Properties) Ltd (1957)**), but why would a mortgagee want to take possession of the property? Well, there are two main reasons. First, possession may be taken as a prelude to sale of the land to meet the mortgage debt. Secondly, possession might also be taken not to sell the land, but to manage the land in order that the debt might be made back in that way.

6.18   Possession can be taken in one of two ways. First, possession might be taken by **peaceful re-entry** or, secondly, by **court order**. Practically, possession is usually taken by court order, especially given the protections it gives to the mortgagor, but peaceful possession is worth mentioning for completeness before we consider possession by court order. Note, possession must be sought only for legitimate reasons and reasonably for the enforcement of the security. Possession which is not in good faith will not be permitted (**Quennell v Maltby (1979)**).

Peaceful possession

6.19   It is possible for the lender to take possession peacefully by re-entering the property, especially where the property is empty, as in **Ropaigealach v Barclays Bank plc (1999)**. By taking possession peacefully, the mortgagee avoids the statutory protections which are given to the mortgagor where possession is taken by court order, as will be seen below. However, the mortgagee must be sure that they do not use force, violence, or threats to effect peaceful possession as this could amount to an offence under s6, Criminal Law Act 1977.

6.20   While, generally, the mortgagee is free to take possession peacefully, there is an important limitation and that is where the mortgagee has taken possession by court order and possession has been suspended by the court using its statutory powers. In that situation, the mortgagee will not then be able to taken possession peacefully (**Goldhill Finance Limited v Cynthia Berry (2018)**).

Possession by Court order

6.21   The most common method of possession is possession by court order. That is, the mortgagee applies to court asking for an order for possession of the mortgaged property. Where an application is made to court for possession, the borrower may attempt to resist the application by asking the court to use its powers under s36, Administration of Justice Act 1970. The provision gives the court a *power* to adjourn the proceedings, or stay or suspend execution of the judgment or postpone the date for possession if the house is: (1) a dwelling or *includes* a dwelling –

so it does not operate for a *wholly* business premises – and (2) it appears the borrower is likely to be able to pay any sums due under the mortgage within a reasonable period. A "reasonable period" is the remainder of the mortgage term (**Cheltenham and Gloucester Building Society v Norgan (1996)**) and the borrower must present a viable financial plan to the court (**National and Provincial Building Society v Lloyd (1996)**).

6.22   A postponement may permit the borrower to sell the property (**Target Home Loans Ltd v Clothier (1994)**), but only where there is clear evidence to support it (**Mortgage Service Funding plc v Steele (1996)**). The court will not generally use the power where the house is in negative equity, that is, where the mortgage debt is greater than the value of the house (**Cheltenham and Gloucester plc v Krausz (1997)**).

(ii) power of sale

6.23   The power of sale must **arise** and become **exercisable**. The power of sale is contained in every mortgage (s101, LPA 1925) and **arises** where the mortgage is by **deed**, the **power is not expressly excluded**, and when the **mortgage money is due**.

6.24   The power only becomes **exercisable** under s103, LPA 1925 where:

(a) notice requiring repayment of capital has been served by the lender *and* the borrower has defaulted for three months after service; or

(b) any interest under the mortgage is in arrears and unpaid for at least two months; or

(c) there has been a breach of some other mortgage provision, either express or implied by the LPA 1925.

6.25   Where the mortgagee exercises the power of sale, the law imposes duties on them in relation to the sale of the property. If those duties are breached, then the mortgagee could be liable to the mortgagor for any losses arising from the breach.

Mortgagee's duties on sale

6.26   When selling the property, the lender is under a duty to take reasonable care to obtain a proper price, dependent on the circumstances of the case (**Newport Farm Ltd v Damesh Holdings Ltd (2003)**), which can mean selling within the appropriate price bracket (**Michael v Miller (2004)**).

6.27   Further, the mortgagee is under a duty to advertise property with any planning permission obtained in relation to the property. This is because land which has planning permission granted has a greater potential value. In **Cuckmere Brick Co Ltd v Mutual Finance Ltd (1971)**, Cuckmere had obtained planning permission to build 35 houses and 100 flats on a piece of land. The power of sale arose and became exercisable, so the mortgagee sold the land at public auction, but only the planning permission for the 35 houses was mentioned in the sale documents.

6.28   The Court of Appeal held that the law imposed duties on the mortgagee when exercising the power of sale. These included a duty to act in good faith in the conduct of the sale; duty to take reasonable care in the conduct of the sale; and a duty to obtain a fair and proper price. These duties had been breached in this case and Mutual Finance was liable to the mortgagor.

6.29   While the mortgagee may be under an obligation to advertise obtained planning permission, it is not under an obligation to pursue a planning permission application, nor is it under an obligation to improve the property prior to sale (**Silven Properties Ltd v Royal Bank of Scotland plc (2003)**).

6.30   Another important issue is **when to sell?** In **Standard Chartered Bank Ltd v Walker (1982)**, the CA said, *obiter*, that the lender had to exercise reasonable care in deciding when to sell, although **Cuckmere Brick Co Ltd v Mutual Finance Ltd (1971)** and **China and South Sea Bank Ltd v Tan Soon Gin (1990)** suggest the contrary; the lender can sell the property when he likes. That said, a sale in haste to satisfy the mortgage debt will not be acceptable (**Predeth v Castle Phillips Finance Co Ltd (1986)**).

6.31   The burden of proving a breach of the mortgagee's duties on sale rests with the mortgagor. The remedy where breach of duty is shown is the difference between the price obtained and the proper market value, though evidence will be needed to support the mortgagor in their claim that the proper market value was not reached. In extreme cases, the court could set aside the claim.

6.32   An interesting case in this area is **Palk v Mortgage Services Funding plc (1993)**, where the lender wanted to ride out the market and wait for an improvement. However, the court permitted the borrower to force sale on the basis that the arrears would have accrued at £30,000 per year imposing a significant burden on the borrower. The mortgagor can seek sale under section 91, LPA 1925.

6.33   Where the sale realises more than the mortgage debt, any surplus is held on trust for the borrower (s105, LPA 1925)).

(iii) appointment of receiver

6.34   A lender might appoint a receiver under a power in s101, LPA 1925. The receiver is appointed to manage or administer the mortgaged property. When appointed, the receiver becomes the borrower's agent, meaning the lender is not liable to the borrower for the receiver's acts. Instead, the receiver is liable to the borrower. An example of this liability in action is the case of **Medforth v Blake (2000)**, where a receiver was appointed by the lender to run a mortgaged pig farm. The receiver was liable for an error in failing to negotiate a discount for the purchase of pig food.

(iv) foreclosure

6.35   This is the remedy of last resort since it seizes all of the borrower's rights and gives them to the lender. Since it has such an extreme impact on the borrower, it may only be granted by court order. It is a remedy little used today, and the Law Commission has recommended it be abolished.

Protection and Enforcement of Mortgages

6.36   As with other interests in land, mortgages are also subject to the schemes of protection of interests in **registered** and **unregistered title**.

Registered Title

6.37   A legal mortgage is a registrable disposition in registered title under s27(2)(f), LRA 2002. This means that even though it is created validly by deed, it needs to be registered to keep its status as a *legal* mortgage. This is done by being a '**registered charge**' on the Charges Register. This appears in two parts in that section of the Register. The first part gives the date and brief details of the charge, while the second part gives the name and address of the registered proprietor, which is usually the bank or building society which is the mortgagee.

6.38   An equitable mortgage should be protected as a Notice on the Charges Register (s32, LRA 2002).

Unregistered Title

6.39   Where title is unregistered, a first legal mortgage is protected by deposit of the title deeds with the mortgagee as security. A second, or subsequent, legal mortgage, known as a puisne (pronounced *puny*) mortgage, must be registered as a C(i) land charge (s2(4)(i), Land Charges Act 1972), an equitable mortgage should be registered as a C(iii) land charge (s2(4), (iii), Land Charges Act 1972). If neither is registered, a Class C land charge will be void against a purchaser of the land unless registered before the completion of the purchase.

Undue Influence

6.40   One topic which operates alongside mortgages is one you should already be familiar with from your study of contract law, and that topic is undue influence. If you cast your mind back to the heady days of contract law, you will recall that undue influence is something which allows a contract to be avoided because the weaker party was pressured unduly into signing the contract. In mortgages, the same is true. A party who feels coerced or pressured into signing the mortgage agreement may be able to avoid enforcement of the mortgage by showing that they were subject to undue influence by another before signing it.

6.41 Much of the modern law on undue influence has come from cases where joint owners of property enter into a joint mortgage, usually to support a failing business, but one party *pressures* the other party to sign the joint mortgage. The question is: can the pressured party avoid the mortgage? The issue is usually approached in three stages:

1 Has the party wishing to avoid the mortgage demonstrated undue influence?	2 If so, was the mortgagee put on inquiry as to the undue influence?	3 If so, did the mortgagee take *reasonable steps* to avoid the notice of undue influence?

6.42 The case which has done more than any other in recent years to clarify the law in this area is **Royal Bank of Scotland v Etridge (No 2) (2001)**. Now, let's start with the first of the questions, above, namely, how does the party wishing to avoid the mortgage demonstrate undue influence?

6.43 There are two categories of undue influence and these are **actual undue influence** and **presumed undue influence**.

Actual undue influence

6.44 In contrast to situations of presumed undue influence, actual undue influence must be proved against a party. This can be tricky because it is frequently one person's word against another. So, for these difficult evidential reasons, if the victim is able to demonstrate the situation is one where undue influence can be presumed, that would be the more sensible option.

Presumed undue influence

6.45   Undue influence is presumed where there is a relationship of **trust and confidence** and the **transaction is one which requires explanation**.

6.46   Let's start with relationships of **trust and confidence**. Some relationships are presumed to be relationships of trust and confidence. Common among such relationships are doctor-patient, solicitor-client,   parent-child,   trustee-beneficiary.   In   other situations, the parties must prove it was a relationship of trust and confidence. A common example of this is the relationship of husband and wife, where the one party has to prove they placed trust and confidence in the other party in financial matters.

6.47   On its own, it is insufficient to prove that the relationship is one of trust and confidence. It is also necessary to demonstrate the second element, namely that the **transaction calls for explanation**. This means that the transaction is one which is not easily explained by the nature of the relationship between the parties *alone*.

6.48   As   a   presumption,   like   most   presumptions,   the presumption of undue influence is one which can be rebutted by evidence that the innocent party had, for example, taken legal advice before the transaction was carried out.

6.49   The second of the questions, above, once undue influence is presumed, asks whether the party seeking to enforce the contract, or in this case the mortgagee seeking to enforce the mortgage, is whether they were ***put on inquiry***. In other words, did the mortgagee have notice of the undue influence? The House of Lords in the case of *Etridge* said that the mortgagee will be on enquiry where, first, **one party is providing security for another's debt**, and, the **relationship between the surety and the debtor is non-commercial**.

6.50   A good example of this might be where the mortgage is for the sole purpose of one party, that is, to support one party's business. Here, a bank might be put on notice. By contrast, the bank might not be put on notice where the mortgage is for a joint purpose, eg, the purchase of a joint holiday home. In **CIBC Mortgages plc v Pitt (1994)**, a mortgagee was not put on notice where the mortgage application stated that it was for the purchase of a holiday home when, in fact, the money was to be used by the husband to speculate on the stock market! Ignoring the potential for mortgage fraud, the bank was not on inquiry because it appeared as a mutually beneficial debt, rather than one person guaranteeing (or providing security) for another person's debt.

6.51 If the bank is, however, put on inquiry (notice), the third question, above, asks whether the mortgagee has taken reasonable steps to satisfy itself that the innocent party has had the seriousness of the transaction, and what it might mean, made clear to them. What does this mean that the mortgagee should do? We'll consider that next.

6.52 In order for a mortgagee to be able to enforce a mortgage, where it is on notice of undue influence, it should follow what has become known as the 'Etridge Protocol'. What is the point? The rationale behind this is that the mortgagee is seeking to avoid a situation where the mortgage is unenforceable by them in the event of a default in payment. Therefore, the mortgagee should take steps to see that the worst, from their point of view, does not happen. So, in the next table, we consider the 'Etridge Protocol' which, if a bank follows it, will be able to enforce the mortgage against the innocent party.

The 'Etridge Protocol'

Mortgagee should do the following to ensure innocent party understands the risks of the proposed transaction

1 Advise the innocent party that they should take independent legal advice from a solicitor

2 Solicitor should meet with the innocent party, ideally face-to-face, without the other party

3 Solicitor should provide written confirmation that advice was given and the transactions explained

4 Innocent party should be told that they are free to refuse to go ahead with the transaction

6.53 The importance of lenders complying with the guidelines from *Etridge* was emphasised in the case of **HSBC Bank plc v Brown (2015)**. Banks are careful, as part of their loan risk management, to see that the 'Etridge Protocol' is followed.

6.54 Successful use of the 'Etridge Protocol' means that the onus shifts from the mortgagee to the legal professional, the solicitor, who provides the advice. However, if the advice is appropriate, then there are no more avenues available to the innocent party and they will have to accept the consequences of signing on the dotted line.

What if the undue influence claim is successful?

6.55 Up to this point, we have focused on what happens if a mortgagee is successful in enforcing the mortgage and avoiding the allegation that the mortgage was extracted by undue influence. But, **what happens if the innocent party is successful in showing that the mortgage *was* extracted by undue influence?** Well, there are two basic options.

6.56   First, it could be that an ***all or nothing*** approach is taken and that the entire agreement is set aside and unenforceable by the mortgagee (**TSB v Camfield (1995)**). However, an alternative is the more balanced approach adopted in the case of **First National Bank plc v Achampong (2003)**.

6.57   In *Achampong*, a husband and wife entered into a joint legal mortgage. The mortgage was set aside for undue influence on the part of the husband who had pressured the wife into signing the mortgage agreement. The court held that the mortgage could be enforced against the husband's interest in the property, but not against the wife who was able to argue undue influence.

6.58   Section 63, LPA 1925 had the effect of severing the interests of the husband and wife which gave rise to an equitable mortgage of the husband's equitable interest. This meant that while the wife could keep her equitable interest, the bank could enforce the equitable mortgage by seeking an order for sale under the statutory provisions in sections 14 and 15, Trusts of Land and Appointment of Trustees Act 1996. For more on ss14 and 15, see chapter eight on 'Trusts of Land'.

6.59   While the wife is unlikely to be able to stay in the house, the approach in *Achampong* strikes a balance by making clear that, in reality, there are two victims. First, the wife who is a victim of undue influence, and, secondly, the bank who thought they were getting security over the whole property, but end up with enforceable security over only half the property.

CHAPTER 7
PROPRIETARY ESTOPPEL

Introduction

7.01   Much of English land law is concerned with the formal acquisition of estates and interests, but there are some ways of **acquiring property rights informally**, and **proprietary estoppel** is one of them.

7.02   Now, before we go on I should say something about estoppel. You will be familiar with it as a concept already as it pops up in every contract law course as *promissory estoppel*. Proprietary estoppel and promissory estoppel are both derived from **equitable estoppel**, but they operate quite differently. Probably the most prominent difference is that **proprietary estoppel is a shield or a sword**. In other words, proprietary estoppel can be used as a **defence (a shield)** or as the basis of a **cause of action (a sword) to bring a claim**. Promissory estoppel, by contrast, is merely a shield.

7.03   In essence, a **proprietary estoppel** arises where one party makes an **assurance** (or similar) about a property right, and the party to whom it is made acts in **reliance** on that assurance to their **detriment**. Once these elements are satisfied, if it is **unconscionable** to deny it, the court has discretion to award a remedy to *satisfy the equity*.

7.04   Thus, the elements of proprietary estoppel are:

(i) An individual makes an **assurance (or representation)**, a **promise**, or **acquiesces** in a misunderstanding, that another will enjoy some right;

(ii) The recipient will then place **reliance** on that assurance, etc;

(iii) Which reliance is **detrimental** to the recipient;

(iv) The maker of the assurance, etc, then acts

unconscionably in seeking to deny the right promised.

Gillett v Holt (2000)(CA); Thorner v Major (2009)(HL)

7.05   Although these elements are cited separately, remember we are dealing with an equitable concept here, so flexibility is key, even in application of the principles (**Taylor Fashions v Liverpool Victoria Trustees Co (1981)**). Consequently, some of these elements may overlap. For example, reliance and detriment can overlap quite heavily.

7.06   Once the elements are present, the court can award a discretionary **remedy to satisfy the equity**. The remedy is discretionary because proprietary estoppel is an equitable concept and equitable remedies are available only at the discretion of the court.

(i)   An individual makes an assurance, etc

7.07   An individual must make some form of assurance (representation) that the person has or will have some right or interest, in this context, in relation to land. The assurance can be one about the freehold estate (**Gillett v Holt (2000)**), or an interest in land, eg, an easement over land (**Crabb v Arun DC (1976)**).

7.08   The assurance can be by words or conduct, so long as it is 'clear enough' (**Thorner v Major (2009)**). General or vague assurances, such as suggesting that the recipient will always have a roof over their head will not be sufficient (**Coombes v Smith (1986)**), though assurances as to the future receipt of property, such as by will, can be sufficient. For example, in **Re Basham (1986)**, an assurance that a step-daughter would inherit a freehold estate from her step-father was a sufficient assurance.

7.09   The examples in the cases discussed so far are good examples of **active assurances**, where one party encourages another to form a belief. However, acquiescence (**passive assurance**) may be enough where the recipient is mistaken or misunderstands, which the other party realises, but does then not correct the recipient (**Ramsden v Dyson (1866)**).

7.10 Fundamentally, the assurance or promise must be sufficiently clear (**Thorner v Major (2009)(HL)**), when looked at objectively (**Gillett v Holt (2002)(CA)**), and may change over the course of the period relevant to the estoppel claim. In the case of **Guest v Guest (2019)**, the High Court upheld a proprietary estoppel claim, even where what the claimant expected to obtain changed from sole ownership of the farm to joint ownership when the claimant's brother started to work on the farm under similar assurances. Vague assurances lacking credibility will not be enough (**Mayor and Burgesses of the Brent London Borough Council v Johnson (2020)**).

7.11 So far, focus has been on assurances and acquiescence. An **assurance (promise)** arises where someone is told they will receive some right in the future, whether by will (**Jennings v Rice (2002)**) or after the passage of time. **Acquiescence** arises where one party is under a misunderstanding, and the other party knows there is a misunderstanding but they allow the party who has misunderstood to act to their detriment on the misunderstanding. The final form of *statement* is a **representation**. A representation is a statement of fact or law relating to an individual's current rights (**Tomlin v Reid (1963)**).

7.12 Whatever the form of statement made, it **must be made before the detrimental reliance (Churchill v Roach (2004))**. On which point, let's take a look at reliance, then detriment.

(ii) The recipient will then place reliance on that assurance, etc

7.13 Once the assurance has been made, the recipient must act in reliance on that assurance, and the **reliance must be reasonable**, and will be judged objectively. In essence, the requirement is the **causal link** between the assurance and what follows (**Gillett v Holt (2000)**).

7.14 Whether the reliance is reasonable will be a question which relies heavily on the facts, but ongoing contractual negotiations (**Haq v Island Homes Housing Association and another (2011)**) and sensitive business relations conducted between professionals, are unlikely to give rise to a proprietary estoppel as reliance may not be reasonable (**Yeoman's Row Management Ltd v Cobbe (2008)**).

7.15   A good example of reasonable reliance in the domestic context comes from the case of **James v James (2018)**. In that case, a father commented to his son that he, the son, *would be farming the land one day*. The court held, in finding against the son, that the reasonable interpretation could not be the one the son had adopted, so his reliance was not reasonable. Those words could not be reasonably interpreted as intending to give the son property rights in the land.

(iii)   Which reliance is detrimental to the recipient

7.16   Importantly, the reliance, as well as being reasonable, has to be **detrimental** to the recipient or, exceptionally, the detriment of another, eg, a husband on which a wife then based a claim (**Matharu v Matharu (1994)**).

7.17   The detriment must be significant, but it can be monetary or, more usually in estoppel cases, some other form of quantifiable non-monetary detriment (**Gillett v Holt (2000)**). Detriment can overlap with the causal element of the reliance requirement giving greater strength to the argument that the assurance caused the recipient to rely to their detriment (**Gillett v Holt (2000)(CA)**; **Cook v Thomas (2010)(CA)**).

7.18   There are many examples from case law for what has been accepted as detrimental to the recipient. For example, where the recipient pays for improvements to the other's property (**Pascoe v Turner (1979)**), or constructs new buildings on the other's land (**Inwards v Baker (1965)**). Alternatively, one party has cared for an individual for no or little payment (**Grundy v Ottey (2003)**), or worked for another for little or no payment for a number of years (**Greasley v Cooke (1980)**; **Gillett v Holt (2000)**).

(iv) The maker of the assurance, etc, then acts unconscionably in seeking to deny the right promised

7.19   Where the elements are made out and the individual who made the assurance then tries to deny the rights to the recipient, this will be regarded as unconscionable and equity will intervene to prevent the wrong from being committed.

7.20   While unconscionability is not, technically, an element of a proprietary estoppel claim, it is a concept which sits at the heart of the doctrine, permeating all its elements (**Taylors Fashions Ltd v Liverpool Victoria Trustees Co. Ltd (1982); Jennings v Rice (2002)**). Importantly, unconscionability is a flexible concept and, as such, the courts could take account of the conduct of any of the parties to the claim in seeking to come to a conclusion on it.

Remedy

7.21   The elements, once made out, **give rise to an equity**, which is **satisfied by the award of a remedy**. The appropriate approach to the remedy in this area of law was reviewed by the Supreme Court in **Guest v Guest (2022)**, where guidelines seem to have been provided. These will be reviewed later, but first some principles which have survived that case.

7.22   Importantly, because we are dealing with an equitable concept in proprietary estoppel, the **remedy is flexible**, allowing the court considerable **discretion** either to award the thing promised, or compensation, or something else. Generally, it is deemed to be the **minimum necessary to do justice (Jennings v Rice (2002))**. This is the embodiment of a recurring theme in the remedies cases, namely proportionality, which is inherent in the Supreme Court's approach in *Guest v Guest*. The remedy should not be out of proportion to the detriment which the claimant has suffered.

7.23   Naturally, because of flexibility, discretion, and proportionality, it is difficult to be definitive on what the court will award, so looking at the cases can provide useful guidance.

7.24   In **Pascoe v Turner (1979)**, the recipient was promised the house, so legal title was transferred to them as the remedy. In **Greasley v Cooke (1980)**, the assurance was that the recipient could remain in a house for the rest of her life, and the court gave her the right to live there for the rest of her life. In **Crabb v Arun DC (1976)**, Crabb was promised a right of access over land he sold to the council, which the council denied after Crabb sold the land. The court upheld the assurance and gave Crabb the right of access. A similar outcome occurred in the case of (**Hoyl Group v Cromer Town Council (2015)**).

7.25   In some circumstances, the recipient will not always get what they expected on the basis of the 'assurance'. In **Jennings v Rice (2002)(CA)**, the court said account should be taken between **expectation** and the **reliance** and that the remedy should be **proportionate** to reflect any difference between the two. Therefore, they awarded £200,000 even though the recipient had been promised a house valued at £435,000. The figure awarded represented the value of the work done by the claimant.

7.26   The approach of giving a figure representing the work done was taken in **Habberfield v Habberfield (2018)**, where a daughter had worked for little or no wages on her father's farm on the assurance she would, one day, receive the farm. The farm was worth more than the value of the recipient's reliance (approximately 10 times more), so she was awarded a sum of money in compensation; the remedy was proportionate. This part of the decision was upheld by the Court of Appeal in 2019.

7.27   In *Guest v Guest*, the Supreme Court appears to have taken the following approach, which embodies an approach already regarded as the appropriate one to take in such cases. First, the court should consider whether the **repudiation by the promisor would be unconscionable**. Unconscionability is, of course, a central theme of equity, and a central theme of proprietary estoppel since the House of Lords in *Thorner v Major*. Secondly, once satisfied it would be unconscionable to repudiate the promise, the court should **consider awarding that which was promised**. This used to be termed giving the promise their expectation. However, the third part limits the enforcement of the promise to the extent of **whether the award of the full**

promise would be out of all proportion to the detriment. Again, the theme of proportionality has been one consistent in case law on the remedies to satisfy the proprietary estoppel.

Protection of an interest by proprietary estoppel

7.28 A proprietary estoppel is capable of binding third parties who purchase land which is subject to the proprietary estoppel. Where title is registered, s116 Land Registration Act 2002 makes the point that such interests are capable of binding third parties. It should be registered as a Notice on the Charges Register of the burdened land (s32, LRA 2002), unless it is an interest which overrides by actual occupation under schedule 3, paragraph 2, LRA 2002. Where title is unregistered, whether a proprietary estoppel is binding is determined by the doctrine of notice (**Ives (ER) Investment Ltd v High (1967)**).

CHAPTER 8
TRUSTS OF LAND

Introduction

8.01   The trust is something you have heard about, but may not be too familiar to you. Of course, you will be when you study trusts, but that may not be for another year. So, we need to address this and tell you about the trust concept and what you read over the next two (and a bit) pages will be **crucial** for the chapters on trusts of the home (chapter nine) and common ownership (chapter 10), so read this once, and if it doesn't go in, read it again.

8.02   When we normally think of ownership, we think of outright ownership. That is, one person owns all the rights to property, whether that property is land or any other kind of property. Now, ownership of any form of property carries with it a bundle of rights and duties. Well, what if I said that English law allows you to split these rights? What if I said that English law allows you to give some of those rights away and keep some for yourself? Well, English law does allow this, and it does it under the trust.

8.03   A trust is an equitable obligation where **legal title is held by a trustee** and **equitable title is held by a beneficiary**. Equitable title is also known as the beneficial title. The use of the trust is quite common in land ownership, especially where land is held jointly by husband and wife, or by civil partners. It can also be used where there is one legal owner and multiple (frequently two) equitable owners. This was common in the past where a married couple put ownership of the matrimonial home in one name, usually the man's name, and the man and the woman owned the house jointly as equitable owners.

8.04   So, what we understand by this is that the same piece of land can be owned by multiple people under this mechanism called the trust. A trust is flexible and can have one legal owner or multiple legal owners (but there is a limit to the number of legal owners, as you will see shortly), and multiple beneficiaries.

8.05   What does this mean practically? Well, *practically*, it means that the legal owner(s) is the person whose name is entered on the Register at the Land Registry, while the equitable owners protect their interest as a Restriction on the Proprietorship Register (s40, LRA 2002), or hope that they satisfy the requirements for their equitable interest to override by actual occupation (sch 3, para 2, LRA 2002).

8.06   What might a trust of land look like? Let's think about this by the use of a couple diagrams.

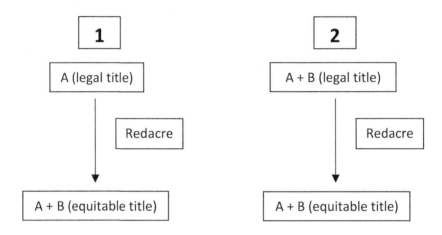

8.07   Here we have two scenarios, 1 and 2. Both scenarios concern trusts of land called Redacre. Same piece of land, owned in two different ways. In scenario 1, A owns the legal title alone. A would be registered at the Land Registry as the Proprietor of Redacre. The equitable ownership is, however, split between A and B. So, in this trust, there is one legal owner and two equitable owners. Effectively, A holds the land on trust for himself and B. A's interest is protected because they are the legal owner, but B would need to protect their equitable interest by a Restriction on the Proprietorship Register (s40, LRA 2002), or hope that they are in actual occupation so their equitable interest is protected as an interest which overrides (sch 3, para 2, LRA 2002).

8.08   In scenario 2, A and B hold the legal title jointly. A and B would be registered at the Land Registry as the Joint Proprietors of Redcare. The equitable ownership is, however, split between A and B. Effectively, A and B hold the land on trust for themselves. Neither A nor B needs to protect their equitable interest because both are registered legal owners.

8.09   Why does it matter? Well, it matters because the equitable ownership is a valuable property right. It can be given away, sold, or even mortgaged. It also matters because the law imposes certain rights and duties on legal and equitable owners of land.

8.10   Finally on these introductory points, a little more by way of background information before we consider the detail of the governing statute, the Trusts of Land and Appointment of Trustees Act 1996.

8.11   English law **limits the number of legal owners of land to no more than four** (s34(2), Trustee Act 1925). There are good practical reasons for this limitation, but they mostly concern land dealing. It is easier to deal with land where there are fewer legal owners. In terms of the number of equitable owners, there is no statutory limit so, *technically*, the number is unlimited. However, English law does impose a form of restriction in that the number of beneficiaries should not be so large so as to make the trust administratively unworkable (**McPhail v Doulton (1970)**). In reality, however, the number of beneficiaries in a trust of land is likely to be small.

8.12   The following cannot be emphasised enough: When a trust of land is created, there is a **separation of ownership between a legal owner(s) and an equitable owner(s)**.

Single Legal Owner

8.13   A single (outright) owner of land may create (declare) a trust and create an equitable interest for another. As shown here, there would be **one legal owner and a different single equitable (or beneficial) owner, or multiple beneficial owners**, for example, where the **legal owner creates (declares) a trust of land with himself and another jointly as equitable ownership**. If he created either trust, he would need to comply with a statutory formality under **s53(1)(b), LPA 1925**, because both would be an **express declaration of a trust of land**. The statutory formality requires that an **express declaration of a trust of land must be evidenced by signed writing**. If this is not complied with, the **declaration will be unenforceable** because the claimant will not have the evidence to prove it.

Joint Legal Owners

8.14 Where land is purchased jointly, eg, by two people, and those people are jointly registered as the legal owners of the land, then the **purchase takes effect as a trust of land**, where both are legal owners, and both are equitable owners, as in scenario 2, explained above. The document which transfers the ownership to both parties is called the TR1 form. On the TR1 form, there is a space to explain how the equitable title is held. It is advisable to complete this part of the form, but it is not compulsory. This generates problems down the line, but we will look at those in chapter nine.

8.15 As I said at the beginning of this chapter, it can do you no harm to go back through the previous three and a bit pages to see that you get it, and if there is any doubt, go back and read again. As I said, understanding these fundamentals is crucial for chapters nine and 10 of this book and your study of land law. However, if you are happy that you have a good understanding, we can now go on to consider the main attraction of this chapter, namely the Trusts if Land and Appointment of Trustees Act 1996 ('ToLATA').

Trusts of Land and Appointment of Trustees Act 1996 ('ToLATA 1996')

8.16 Trusts which contain land as any part of the trust property, are **trusts of land** and governed by the provisions of ToLATA. It came into force on 1ˢᵗ January 1997, but applies to all trusts whenever they were created (ss2(1), 2(3), ToLATA).

8.17 The Act confers **powers on the trustees in relation**

to land, **rights on the beneficiaries**, and wide **powers on the courts**. So, if you are concerned with a trust of land, you will come into contact with ToLATA at some stage.

Trustees' Powers in relation to land

8.18   The trustees are given all the powers of an absolute owner. In other words, they have the same powers of a person who owns the land outright. This means that the land can be used for a beneficiary to live in (s6, ToLATA), but the powers under s6, ToLATA may be amended or excluded by the document which creates the trust.

Beneficiaries' Rights in relation to land

8.19   A beneficiary of full age, sound mind, and with an interest under the trust which is in possession must be consulted by the trustees. An interest in possession is one which they enjoy now, not at some point in the future. The consultation is in relation to the exercise of powers, etc, and the trustees must give effect to the wishes of the beneficiaries where they comply with the trust as a whole (s11, ToLATA).

8.20   Where there is a dispute between the beneficiaries, it should be resolved by majority determined by ownership rights. Obviously, in a situation where there are two equal equitable (beneficial) owners, usually in a marriage of civil partnership, there is the potential for 'deadlock', especially where the parties are separating. That said, 'deadlock' can be resolved by the court exercising its powers.

8.21   Naturally, the beneficiary under a trust is entitled to occupy the land (s12, ToLATA), though this may be restricted by reference to the trust terms. In most cases this is what commonly happens where a couple jointly owns a home and occupy it as the matrimonial home. Indeed, the parties won't even consider that they are exercising their rights as beneficiaries under statute, but that is what they are, in fact, doing.

Courts' Powers under ToLATA

8.22   The court has extremely wide powers under ToLATA (**Bagum v Hafiz (2015)**), provided the powers are engaged by an application from a *person with an interest under a trust of land* (14, ToLATA). This could be a trustee, a beneficiary, a mortgagee (if a mortgage had been granted over the land), or the trustee in bankruptcy of a bankrupt beneficiary.

8.23   The nature of the order which the court makes is only really limited by the imagination of the judge, since the court may make such order as **it thinks fit in relation to the trustees' exercise of their functions**, and **the nature and extent of a person's interest in the trust property**.

8.24   When considering a s14 application, the court must have regard to the s15 criteria in making its determination. The criteria under s15(3), ToLATA are:

(a) the intentions of the person(s) who created the trust;

(b) the purposes for which the trust property is to be held. For example, sale will not be ordered where the original purpose still exists (**Re Buchanan-Wollaston's Conveyance (1939)**).

(c) the welfare of any minor who occupies or might reasonably be expected to occupy any land as his home;

(d) the interests of any secured creditor of any beneficiary.

8.25   Under s15(3), ToLATA, the circumstances and wishes of any beneficiaries of full age and, where in dispute, those of the 'majority' are considered. As indicated, this isn't much use where the beneficiaries are 'deadlocked'. The criteria and relevant case law under section 15 are discussed in detail in chapter 10.

8.26   The most common form of order applied for under s14 is an **order for sale**, but they could make an order compelling the physical division of land between the co-owners (**Ellison v Cleghorn (2013)**). Really, section 14 gives the power to make any order necessary to deal with the application.

Occupation rent

8.27   Under ToLATA, the court may award occupation rent (which used to be known as equitable accounting), to a beneficiary who has been excluded from the house which they have a right to occupy. This happened in the cases of **Stack v Dowden (2007)** and **Jones v Kernott (2011)**, which will be looked at in chapter nine.

CHAPTER 9
TRUSTS OF THE HOME

Introduction

9.01 Trusts of the home has undergone radical judicial reform since the decisions of the House of Lords in **Stack v Dowden (2007)** and the Supreme Court in **Jones v Kernott (2011)**. In light of these cases, the question of home ownership can now be approached more flexibly than in the past.

Background

9.02 If married or in a civil partnership, statute confers broad discretionary powers on judges to resolve questions of ownership of property, namely the Matrimonial Causes Act 1973 and the Civil Partnerships Act 2004, respectively. But what happens when couples are not in a formal relationship, buy a house together, but later separate? Or, what happens when the parties get together and one moves into a house which the other owns?

9.03 This is an important social question because an increasing number of couples are neither getting married nor entering into a civil partnership so the solution to the problem English law provides has to be one which is fit for purpose. In that case, how does English law provide a solution? Well, it uses the trust. In fact, it doesn't just use the trust, it has had to manipulate the trust to meet the needs of a changing society.

9.04 Before we get into the detail of the cases in this area – and there are a **lot** of cases – we have to consider the starting point. The starting point is to rely on the distinction placed in English law between those cases where both parties are registered as the legal owners, so-called **joint names cases**, from those where only one of the parties is registered as the owner, namely, **single name cases**. That is how the rest of the discussion will flow.

Express Declaration: Joint Names

9.05   When land is transferred to a couple as **joint legal owners**, then **part 10** of the **TR1 land transfer form** should be completed. Part 10 provides the parties with an opportunity to declare their equitable ownership. They can be (a) **joint tenants**, (b) **tenants in common in equal shares**, or, (c) **hold it another way as they may stipulate**, where the parties can indicate their individual shares. If this is done, then the transferees must sign the TR1 form in order to comply with the requirements of section 53(1)(b), LPA 1925 (**Ralph v Ralph (2021)(CA)**). You will recall that section 53(1)(b), LPA 1925 is the statutory formality relating to declarations of a trust of land. The section provides that, in order to be valid, there must be signed written evidence of the trust. The completion of part 10 of the TR1 with the signatures of the transferees will comply with that requirement.

9.06   Where part 10 of the TR1 is completed, it will be binding, even where one party has provided all the purchase money, but the property is conveyed to them as 'joint tenants' (**R v Hayes (2018)(CA)**). Indeed, all that will negative any declaration under part 10 is a finding of fraud, mistake, undue influence, or proprietary estoppel.

9.07   There is, however, a problem and that problem is that it is **not compulsory to complete part 10 of the TR1**. Baroness Hale in **Stack v Dowden (2007)(HL)** considered it should be compulsory. Indeed, she is not the first judge to bemoan the failure to make compulsory the completion of part 10. If you want to see a judge 'shout' in a judgment, with the statement in upper case letters, take some time to read the immensely entertaining paragraph 44 of Ward LJ's judgment in **Carlton v Goodman (2002)(CA)**. Thank me later.

Express Declaration: Single Name

9.08   Where there is a **single legal owner**, ie, only one name is registered, a declaration of an express trust in favour of the non-legal owner would need to comply with **section 53(1)(b), Law of Property Act 1925**. This requires that the declaration be

evidenced by signed writing. If this occurs, then the non-legal owner will have an enforceable equitable (beneficial) interest. This could be done at the date of the conveyance or at a later date. In fact, where one party moves into a house owned by the other party, it will *always* be at a later date.

9.09 An express declaration is *generally* conclusive (**Pettitt v Pettitt (1969)**; **Goodman v Gallant (1986)**). In the case of **Pankhania v Chandegra (2012)**, the court declined to set aside an express trust unless there was **fraud, mistake, undue influence**, or, in the case of **Clarke v Meadus (2010)**, **proprietary estoppel**.

9.10 If there is no express declaration of trust, the **implied trust (Hodgson v Marks (1971))** or **proprietary estoppel** offer alternative solutions. The implied trust needs no statutory formality since it is exempt by reason of s53(2), LPA 1925.

Implied Trusts

9.11 Two forms of implied trust are relevant for the rest of our discussion: the **resulting trust** and the **constructive trust**. It is worthwhile taking some time to think about such trusts.

Resulting Trust

9.12 The **presumed resulting trust** used to play a significant role in allowing a party to establish an equitable interest in the home. This would arise where one party **provided the purchase money at the point of acquisition** but, for whatever reason, the legal title to the property would go into another's name. The party providing the purchase money would receive a beneficial interest in the land (**Bull v Bull (1955)**).

9.13 However, the presumption of a resulting trust came in for criticism in the family home context because of its **focus on financial contributions**, ignoring all other contributions that go to making a *house a home*. Given this, the House of Lords in **Stack v Dowden (2007)** and the Supreme Court in **Jones v Kernott**

(2011) stated that the presumption of a resulting trust is **not appropriate in the domestic family home context**.

9.14 That being said, the resulting trust still has use in other scenarios, especially where the context is more **commercial** and less **domestic**. For example, where a house purchase was made by members of the same family for purposes of a buy-to-let investment (**Laskar v Laskar (2008)(CA)**), the resulting trust analysis was applied. This stands to reason because a buy-to-let is an investment property, so commercial in nature, even if the parties are related. It will also continue to apply where an agreement is made on the understanding that though the property goes into one party's name, the other party is intended to be beneficially entitled (**Tahir v Faizi (2019)**).

9.15 The courts now seem clear on the difference in approach between domestic and commercial contexts. This is understandable since Baroness Hale reminds us in *Stack* that in law, *context is everything*. The case of **Akinola v Oyadore (2020)**, applying *Laskar*, emphasisd the importance of the distinction drawn in the law between domestic and commercial contexts. The court in *Akinola* also placed reliance on **Geary v Rankine (2010)**, drawing assistance from the approach to the purchase of property for investment purposes set out by Lewison LJ in *Geary*.

9.16 While it seems that the resulting trust has no use in the domestic family home context, it retains some value in the business or investment context of land purchase. That being said, I will provide one footnote and that is the decision of the Privy Council in **Marr v Collie (2017)**. Yes, it is Privy Council and not, therefore, technically binding on the English courts, but the Board did comment that the resulting trust could still have a useful role where the parties are in a domestic relationship, but have made unequal contributions to the purchase price of property and do not have a discernible common intention that the joint beneficial ownership should reflect their joint legal ownership. But, as it stands, *Marr* is out of line with the majority of cases.

Constructive Trust

9.17   The constructive trust, though not traditionally used as a means of informally allocating ownership of the family home, began to be turned to this use in the middle of the 20th century. It has since been stretched as a concept but is now the principal mechanism used in this area of law, at least in the domestic context of home ownership.

Joint Names

9.18   If joint legal owners of land fail to declare how the beneficial interests are held, by filling out part 10 of the TR1 (see 9.05 – 9.07, above), the starting point is **joint beneficial ownership** between the parties (**Stack v Dowden (2007)**; **Jones v Kernott (2011)**). **Both parties have an equal (50:50) equitable interest because they have a legal interest. Joint beneficial ownership is a presumption** which can be rebutted. Rebutting the presumption is difficult (per Lord Walker in **Stack v Dowden (2007)**), but it may be done at two stages:

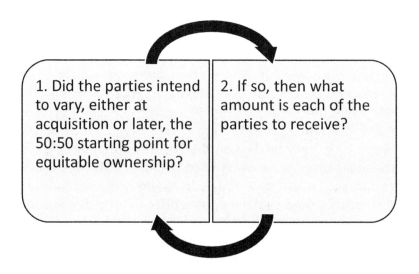

1. Did the parties intend to vary, either at acquisition or later, the 50:50 starting point for equitable ownership?

2. If so, then what amount is each of the parties to receive?

9.19   This two-stage approach was approved by the Court of

Appeal in the case of **Barnes v Phillips (2015)**.

Common intention to vary 50:50?

9.20   To determine if the common intention of the parties has changed, either at the point of acquisition *or* subsequently, the task is to look for the *actual* **intention** of the parties to vary 50:50, or to infer from their conduct a common intention to vary 50:50, either initially or subsequently.

9.21   In **Jones v Kernott (2011)**, the parties cashed in life insurance policies so Mr Kernott could afford to move out of the family home and purchase his own house. From that point, Ms Jones made all the payments in respect of the joint home, ie, the mortgage, the utility bills, and so on. Thus, the common intention varied at that later date.

9.22   Also, in **Barnes v Phillips (2015)(CA)**, a subsequent remortgage was entirely to the benefit of Mr Barnes and that after 2008, Ms Phillips made all the mortgage payments. Thus, it could be inferred from their conduct that there was a common intention to vary 50:50 ownership.

9.23   The factors relevant to determining changes in the common intention of the parties are set down in paragraph 69 of Baroness Hale's speech in **Stack v Dowden (2007)**:

- Advice received by the parties, or discussions which they had at the point of purchase;

- The purpose for which the property was purchased;

- Their motivation for purchasing the property jointly;

- The nature of the relationship between the parties;

- Whether there are children of the relationship for which the parties have a responsibility to provide a home;

- The way in which the parties arranged their finances, eg, did they have separate bank accounts?;

- The way in which the couple paid bills and other outgoings in relation to the property;

- Why one party was authorised to give a valid receipt for capital monies.

9.24 All these factors are equal, where one is not superior to another. However, in some cases, like **Stack v Dowden (2007)**, the courts have given significant weight to financial contributions in departing from 50:50, though the facts of that case are unique. In contrast, in **Fowler v Barron (2008)**, one party contributed nothing towards the purchase of the property either in terms of a deposit or mortgage payments, yet the court did **not** allow the presumption of joint beneficial ownership to be rebutted.

9.25 Before moving on, something should be said about **detriment in joint names cases**. As you will see, detriment plays a significant role in single name cases. However, in joint names cases both parties are deemed to have an interest because of joint legal ownership, with the only question being whether the starting point of 50:50 has been varied by looking at the *Stack* paragraph 69 criteria.

9.26 So, is detriment necessary in joint names cases? Well, the case law is split on the matter. In **O'Neill v Holland (2020)(CA)**, the court rejected the argument that there was no need to establish detriment, but *O'Neill* was a sole name case. By contrast, in **Hudson-v-Hathway (2022)**, the judge felt that detriment was not necessary to establish a varied common intention since the need for detriment was referred to in neither *Stack v Dowden* nor *Jones v Kernott*, which the judge was satisfied was not an oversight in those cases.

What amount is each party to receive?

9.27 One should start the inquiry as to how much by considering if it can be worked out from the actual or inferred (drawing on the factors in para 69 of Stack v Dowden (2007)) common intention of the parties. If not, then it is possible to

impute their fair share having regard to their whole course of dealing in relation to the property. An **imputed intention** is one the parties never actually had, but is one which the court believes is fair (**Jones v Kernott (2011)**, approving **Oxley v Hiscocks (2004)(CA)**). This approach was confirmed by the Court of Appeal in **Barnes v Phillips (2015)**.

9.28   Imputing a share based on what is fair has been criticised as arbitrary and tending to produce inconsistencies (**Aspden v Elvy (2012)**), but it now seems reasonably well-established.

Single Name

9.29   Where one name is on the legal title, the presumption is that the legal owner owns the entire equitable (beneficial) interest: **one legal owner, one beneficial owner**. A party claiming an interest (that is, the non-legal owner) will need to do two things:

a)   Show that they have an interest in the land ('*acquisition issue*'); AND,

b)   The size of that interest ('*quantification issue*').

9.30   This can be done by showing an express declaration of trust to comply with s53(1)(b), LPA 1925 (see, paras 9.08 – 9.10, above), or demonstrating that an implied trust exists, because s53(2), LPA 1925 suspends the formalities of s53(1)(b), LPA 1925 for such trusts. The two forms of implied trust are the resulting trust and the constructive trust, mentioned above at 9.11 – 9.17.

9.31   As indicated, the resulting trust has a limited role in the domestic family home context (**Stack v Dowden (2007)**; **Jones v Kernott (2011)**), though it seems to remain for other commercial situations (**Laskar v Laskar (2008)**). Consequently, we are really only concerned with the **constructive trust**.

9.32   For our purposes, there are two types of constructive trust: *express* **common intention constructive trust**

('**ECICT**'); and, *inferred* **common intention constructive trust** ('**ICICT**') (**Lloyd's Bank v Rosset (1991)**).

9.33   Over the course of the next pages, we'll look at both the ECICT and the ICICT from the perspective of the *acquisition issue* and the *quantification issue* in each case.

'acquisition issue': ECICT

9.34   The ECICT requires two things:

(i)   Express agreement, arrangement, or understanding in relation to ownership of the land; AND

(ii)   Detrimental reliance by the non-legal owner on the agreement, etc.

9.35   The express agreement as to ownership should be at the time of the purchase or *exceptionally* at some later date (**Lloyds Bank v Rosset (1991)**) and communicated between the parties (**Springette v Defoe (1992)**). The agreement has to relate to **ownership of the land**, not merely sharing it as a home. Therefore, in **Clough v Killey (1996)**, a statement that everything was shared '50:50' was sufficient, as was a commitment that everything was 'half yours' in **Hammond v Mitchell (1992)**. Assurances neither understood by *both* parties nor intended as a promise that the non-legal owner will receive an interest will not satisfy the requirement (**James v Thomas (2007)(CA)**).

9.36   Somewhat unusually, the courts have also allowed 'excuses' made by the legal owner to constitute an agreement. In such cases, the legal owner will make an excuse for *not* putting the non-legal owner on the legal title. For example, stating that the non-legal owner is 'too young' as in **Eves v Eves (1974)**, that any inclusion might prejudice a divorce settlement, as in **Grant v Edwards (1986)**, or that there are tax implications from being on legal title as in **Hammond v Mitchell (1992)**. In **Curran v Collins (2015)**, where the excuse related to the expense of two names being on the legal title, the court indicated that interpretation of the excuse is fact-sensitive, but should generally be coupled with a *positive assertion* **the property would be jointly owned.**

9.37 The express agreement should be *followed by* **detrimental reliance (Lloyds Bank v Rosset (1991); Eves v Eves (1974)).** This is conduct which cannot otherwise be explained: why did they do it if they didn't think they were getting an interest in the property? **(Grant v Edwards (1986)).**

9.38 Detriment includes improvements to the family home **(Eves v Eves (1970))**, or indirect financial contributions to the household, without which, alone, the legal owner could not pay the mortgage **(Grant v Edwards (1986)**; and, also, in the ICICT context **(Le Foe v Le Foe (2001))**. Minor amendments and decoration **(Pettitt v Pettitt (1970))** do not count as detrimental reliance.

'quantification issue': ECICT

9.39 Where there is an express agreement which makes clear the share each party is to have, *generally* that will be given effect. So, in **Clough v Killey (1992)** and **Hammond v Mitchell (1992)**, the parties were given half each because that was what was agreed. In **Williamson v Sheikh (2008)**, the court used an unsigned trust deed to determine the agreed share. However, where there has been express agreement as to ownership, but no statement as to the shares, it may be possible to infer an agreement. In **Gallarotti v Sebastianelli (2012)**, two friends bought a property together with an express agreement as to 50:50. This was *later varied by inference* that they were to share the property other than equally where S was awarded a greater share (75%) to account for the fact that S paid the mortgage contributions on his own.

9.40 Where there is no expressly agreed share, and it is not possible to infer from their conduct, then it may be possible for the court to *impute* shares where it is considered **fair having regard to the whole course of dealing between them in relation to**

the property.

'acquisition issue': ICICT

9.41   Where there is no express common intention, it is possible to drawn an **inference to share ownership from the parties' conduct in relation to the property**. In **Lloyds Bank v Rosset (1991)**, Lord Bridge indicated that *only* contributions to mortgage payments would be sufficient to give rise to the inference, *doubting* that anything less than that would do. However, Baroness Hale in **Stack v Dowden (2007)** stated that set the threshold too high and that the **law had moved on** from that position.

9.42   It is possible that indirect financial contributions are sufficient if they are referable to the acquisition of the property (**Gissing v Gissing (1968)**). Also, where the contributions are to payment of bills, without which, the legal owner would not be able to afford the mortgage, then this may suffice (**Le Foe v Le Foe (2001)**). This is sometimes referred to as the 'family economy thesis'.

9.43   Further, substantial improvement to the property by DIY might be enough to infer an agreement to share ownership (*obiter* in **Stack v Dowden (2007)**). Also, in **Aspden v Elvy (2012)**, an inference was found where the direct financial contributions were made to the conversion of the property, rather than to its acquisition.

9.44   Perhaps the most significant development is the suggestion in the Privy Council case of **Abbott v Abbott (2007)** that the full range of paragraph 69 factors from **Stack v Dowden (2007)** (see, para 9.23, above), might be used when seeking to draw an inference as to sharing ownership of the home.

9.45   Before turning to the issue of quantification, it is worth noting that it is **not possible to impute at this stage** in the process, ie, 'acquisition' (**Capethorn v Harris (2015)(CA)**).

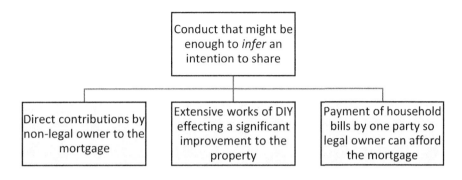

9.46 The alternatives in the diagram, above, are indicated in the case law, but there may be other approaches as the law develops, particularly if the comments in the Privy Council in *Abbott* are embraced. While that might be welcome in an area like this one, recent notes of caution should be highlighted.

9.47 In **Morris v Morris (2008)**, the Court of Appeal was keen to show that an inferred common intention constructive trust will only arise, from the review of the cases, in **exceptional circumstances**. Indeed, efforts by the non-legal owner in relation to the running of a business with the legal owner as in Morris, and, also, in the earlier case of **James v Thomas (2007)**, are unlikely to be sufficiently *exceptional* to given rise to the necessary inference. This is so even where the work is, *apparently*, extensive as in *James* where the non-legal owner drove a tipper, dug trenches, collected materials, laid concrete, tarmac, and gravel, and undertook manual work, collectively described in the claim as Herculean, but insufficient to give rise to an inference.

9.48 While the approach in *Morris* and *James* is, perhaps, understandable. Both hold that the work should *relate* to the land in which one is seeking to establish an interest, and not necessarily in the legal owners' business. However, this is a narrowing of the approach of the courts when it comes to the circumstances which might give rise to an inference to share.

'quantification issue': **ICICT**

9.49 Generally, the inference will generate the amount to be shared. So, if the inference is equality, that will be the position.

However, if nothing can be inferred, then, and only then, may the court impute by **having regard to the whole course of dealing between the parties in relation to the property (Oxley v Hiscocks (2004)**, approved in **Jones v Kernott (2011))**. This approach was taken in **Thompson v Hurst (2012)**, **Aspden v Elvy (2012)**, and **Graham-York v York (2015)**.

Proprietary Estoppel

9.50   A further means of establishing an interest in the home and which was certainly in prominent use prior to the changes made to the law by **Stack v Dowden (2007)** and **Jones v Kernott (2011)**, is proprietary estoppel. Prior to the changes brought about by *Stack* and *Jones*, proprietary estoppel offered a basis for reforming the law in this area (**Law Commission, Sharing Homes: Discussion Paper, Law Com No 278 (2002)**). There is more detail in **chapter seven on proprietary estoppel**.

Reform

9.51   It is certainly the case that the law has been significantly reformed by judicial action since the decision of the House of Lords in **Stack v Dowden (2007)**, but is this the end of the matter? Possibly not. There has been an increase in cases before the courts since *Stack* as its limits are explored in order to produce settled principles. However, an approach which has 'fairness' in it will always result in some degree of uncertainty in case law, though it is doubtful a comprehensive statutory regime would produce a system which is any better as it would still need to be discretionary. This is the problem with an area of law such as this one. Legal rules and principles which are too strict may result in some semblance of injustice, as in **Burns v Burns (1984)**, whereas a system which places reasonable discretion in the hands of the judiciary may be difficult to apply consistently from case to case.

CHAPTER 10
COMMON OWNERSHIP

Introduction

10.01 Co-ownership (Common Ownership) arises where property is owned by at least two people. Most types of property might be co-owned, eg, a bank account (**Paul v Constance (1977)**), or a car, but in English law, co-ownership is examined in detail in relation to **joint ownership of land**. Therefore, co-ownership in land law occurs where two or more people own title to land, whether legal ownership, equitable ownership, or both.

Types of Co-ownership

10.02 In relation to land, co-ownership may operate either where land is owned **successively** or **concurrently**.

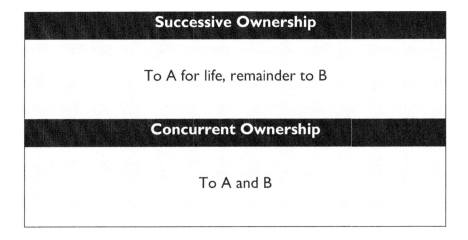

Successive Ownership
To A for life, remainder to B

Concurrent Ownership
To A and B

10.03 Where land is owned **successively**, as in the first example, A will be able to live in the house for life, while B (or B's estate) will be able to enjoy the property when A dies. The interests are **successive interests** because one exists after the other. In the second example, A and B have **concurrent interests**. This means that each has the right to occupy the land at the same time, meaning their interests exist concurrently. Land owned jointly by husband and wife, or by civil partners is commonly owned in this way. The successive interest ownership model is something you will be more concerned with when you study equity and trusts law.

Basics of Co-ownership

10.04   Since 1st January 1997, the date on which the Trusts of Land and Appointment of Trustees Act ('ToLATA') 1996 came into force, all **co-owned land takes effect as a trust of land**. Where a trust is imposed, there is a **separation of legal and equitable title**. **Legal title** is owned by the **trustee**, while **equitable title** is owned by the **beneficiary**. In many of the trusts we are concerned with in this chapter, the trustees and beneficiaries are frequently the same people. So, a married couple will own the land as trustees on trust for themselves as beneficiaries. If you want to be reminded in detail of this content, look back at chapter eight.

10.05   Co-owned land might be held as a **joint tenancy** or a **tenancy in common**. While **legal title might only be held as a joint tenancy** (s1(6), Law of Property Act ('LPA') 1925) and by a **maximum** of **four legal owners** (s34(2), Trustee Act 1925; s34(2), LPA 1925), **equitable title** might be held as a **joint tenancy** or **tenancy in common**, and is capable of having many owners, though probably not so many that it would be administratively unworkable to manage the trust (**McPhail v Doulton (1970)(HL)**). Now, what are these concepts of the **joint tenancy** and **tenancy in common**? They are crucial to this chapter, so let's get these straight in our heads before we go any further.

10.06   A **joint tenancy** exists where multiple owners are treated **as if they are one person** owning the land. Crucial to the joint tenancy is the existence of the four unities (**AG Securities v Vaughan (1990)(HL)**). The **'four unities'** are Possession, Interest, Title and Time.

Possession	Each co-owner is as entitled to possession of each and every part of the land as any other. Unity of possession is the only unity present in both a joint tenancy and a tenancy in common.
Interest	Each joint tenant must have the same interest in nature, eg, a freehold title and duration, eg, a fee simple.
Title	Each joint tenant must acquire title from the same document or by the same act. Therefore, rights acquired under the same conveyance, or by simultaneous possession will suffice.
Time	Each joint tenant's interest must vest, ie, take effect, at the same time.

10.07   It is important to note that all four unities must be present for a joint tenancy to exist. However, **unity of possession** is the only unity which is present in a **joint tenancy** and a **tenancy in common**.

10.08   Another important feature of the **joint tenancy** is the **right of survivorship** (*jus accrescendi*). As joint tenants are treated as if one person, where one dies, they are unable to pass their interest under their will, nor will it pass on intestacy (Administration of Estates Act 1925), but instead it **accrues to the remaining joint tenants (Re Caines (1978))**. Let's consider that by way of an example.

10.09   A, B, and C are joint tenants at law and in equity of Redacre, a house. Yesterday, C died in a car accident. His will, which was validly executed, left all his property to D. D will inherit all of C's property **except** C's interest in Redacre because C was a joint tenant of Redacre along with A and B. Therefore, C's interest in Redcare accrues, that is, stays with Redacre's joint tenants (now A and B), and D inherits all of C's other property. So, A and B are now joint tenants in law and equity of Redacre and D has no interest in it.

10.10 Please note, while there is no formality to change the equitable ownership, A and B should *technically* complete a 'Deceased Joint Proprietor ('DJP')' and send it to the Land Registry to inform them of the death of a joint legal owner. The DJP form can only be used when there is still at least one surviving owner of the property. The Land Registry will remove the name of the deceased joint owner as a proprietor of the title.

10.11 A **tenancy in common** exists where each of the co-owners has an **identifiable share, but it is undivided from the whole**, ie, '**an undivided share**'. While the four unities are necessary for a joint tenancy to exist, only unity of possession is necessary for a tenancy in common.

10.12 In contrast to a joint tenancy, because a tenant in common has an identifiable, yet undivided share of the land, the interest can be left under a will and it will be effective, provided the will is validly executed (s9, Wills Act 1837). Equally, where there is no will, the rules on intestacy will operate to take the share to the next of kin of the deceased (Administration of Estates Act 1925).

10.13 So, to change the facts of the example given at 10.09, above, let's say that C was a tenant in common of $1/3^{rd}$ of Redacre when he died and his will left all his property to D. D would not only inherit all the property that he originally inherited, but he would also inherit the $1/3^{rd}$ interest in Redacre. Therefore, D would be a co-owner of Redacre alongside A and B.

10.14 So, should you wish to avoid the consequences of the right of survivorship, you would need to be a tenant in common of the land and not a joint tenant.

Summary comparison – joint tenancy and tenancy in common	
Joint tenancy	Tenancy in Common
- Treated as owning the whole property as a single person - Four unities must be present - Right of survivorship applies on death of a joint tenant	- Own an identifiable but undivided share in the property - Only unity of possession is needed - Right of survivorship does not apply

Is there a Joint Tenancy or Tenancy in Common?

10.15 Well, legal title is easy, since this is **always a joint tenancy** (s1(6), LPA 1925), so it is never an issue how legal title is held. It follows from this that a joint tenancy at law cannot be severed (s36(2), LPA 1925). One final thing, remember that the legal title can only be held by a **maximum** of **four legal owners** (s34(2), Trustee Act 1925; s34(2), LPA 1925).

10.16 More complicated is **equitable title**, since this can be held as a **joint tenancy or a tenancy in common**. Thankfully, there are a number of things which you can look at to decide whether equitable title is a joint tenancy or a tenancy in common and these are: **whether the four unities are present; whether there is an express declaration; where words of severance are used**; and, **whether a presumption operates**.

Four Unities

10.17 Where the four unities of possession, interest, title and time are present, the equitable title will be held as a joint tenancy.

Express Declaration

10.18 Where the land is transferred to the parties and it expressly states that the equitable ownership takes effect as a joint tenancy or a tenancy in common, then that will be conclusive (**Goodman v Gallant (1986)**; **Pink v Lawrence (1977)**). As a general rule, the only things which will change the conclusive nature of express words is if the party seeking to avoid it is able to prove mistake, fraud, or undue influence (**Pankhania v Chandegra (2012)**).

Words of Severance

10.19 Where the conveyance contains words of severance, a tenancy in common in equity may be found. Words of severance might be, eg, 'in equal shares' (**Payne v Webb (1874)**) or 'equally' (**Re Kilvert (1957)**). Again, they would have the same effect as the express declaration and conclusive of a tenancy in common.

Presumptions

10.20 Equity operates a presumption against the joint tenancy since it *dislikes* the joint tenancy. Therefore, where property is purchased with unequal contributions of money, a tenancy in common will be found (**Bull v Bull (1955)**).

10.21 Alternatively, where the relationship is a business, a tenancy in common will be found (**Lake v Craddock (1732); Bathurst v Scarborow (2004)**).

10.22 Finally, where there is nothing else to go on, the maxim *equity follows the law* operates. So, if there are joint legal owners, then equity presumes a joint tenancy, especially in the domestic context of the shared home (**Stack v Dowden (2007); Jones v Kernott (2011)**).

10.23 Of course, presumptions can be rebutted. So, in **R v Hayes (2018)(CA)**, the fact that one party provided all the purchase money, similar to the situation in *Bull v Bull* at para 10.20, above, did not stop the court finding, based on contrary evidence, that there was a joint tenancy in equity.

10.24 The discussion which we've just had is the starting point. It provides the basis for ownership in commonly owned land. We're now going to move on to discuss another important element of co-ownership and that is the **severance of the joint tenancy in equity**. This **turns the equitable joint tenancy into a tenancy in common**. Remember, *it is only possible to sever a joint tenancy in equity. A joint tenancy at law cannot be severed.*

Severance

10.25 Where a joint tenancy exists in equity, the right of survivorship operates to remove the possibility that a joint tenant might leave his interest by will on death (**Re Caines (1978)**). Therefore, in order to **defeat the right of survivorship**, the **parties must sever the joint tenancy and become tenants in common (Harris v Goddard (1983))**.

10.26 When a joint tenant severs in equity, it impacts only their interest. Other joint tenants remain as joint tenants.

Before severance	*After severance*
A, B, C (JTs in Law)	A, B, C (JTs in Law)
A, B, C (JTs in Equity)	A, B (JTs) | C (TiC 1/3rd)

10.27 In this example, before severance we see that A, B, and C are joint tenants at law and in equity. However, C then decides to sever the equitable joint tenancy. They validly sever and become a tenant in common (TiC) of one-third (which is calculated by dividing between the number of joint tenants). A and B remain joint tenants (JTs) because C severed their interest, so A and B are unaffected. This means that the right of survivorship would still operate between A and B, but not to C, who is now a tenant in common. Note that the legal ownership is unaffected by the severance.

10.28 There are number of ways an equitable joint tenancy might be severed. Where equitable title is severed, the proportions are taken equally (**Goodman v Gallant (1986)(CA)**), unless the parties have contributed in unequal shares (**Bull v Bull (1955)(CA)**; **Stack v Dowden (2007)(HL)**), or agreed to some other form of division. Where severance is successful, it only severs the interest of the party severing. However, where there are only two joint tenants, and one severs, the whole of the joint tenancy is severed since the remaining party cannot be a joint tenant alone. Severance might be effected by:

> 1. Statutory written notice to other joint tenants (s36(2), LPA 1925);
>
> 2. Common law methods ('such other acts or things'):
>
> > (i) An act operating on its share;
> >
> > (ii) Mutual agreement;
> >
> > (iii) Mutual conduct/course of dealing.
>
> 3. Forfeiture as a means of severance.

1. Statutory written notice to other joint tenants

10.29   Under s36(2), LPA 1925 a joint tenant might sever the equitable estate by giving express written notice to the other joint tenants of their desire to sever the joint tenancy. The **written notice must manifest an immediate and irrevocable intention to sever (Re Draper's Conveyance (1969))**. An intention to sever at some point in the future will not suffice (**Harris v Goddard (1983)(CA)**). No particular form of words is needed, nor is the notice required to be signed.

10.30   The cases of *Re Draper's Conveyance* and *Harris v Goddard* are instructive of the level of certainty and intention accepted by the courts. Both cases concerned divorce. In *Re Draper's*, the wife issued divorce proceedings seeking an order that the joint matrimonial home be sold and the proceeds to be divided equally between the husband and wife. This was an effective severance because it was an *immediate and irrevocable* intention to sever.

10.31   By contrast, in *Harris v Goddard*, the wife's petition merely asked for a 'just' order in relation to the matrimonial home. The court held that this was insufficient to sever the joint tenancy so that when the husband died a few days before the hearing, the joint tenancy was not severed and the husband's interest in the house accrued to the wife by survivorship.

10.32 In order to be valid, the written notice under s36(2) must also be correctly served. Under s196, LPA 1925 certain conditions attach to correct service of the written notice. Under s196(3), LPA 1925, in order for service to be effective, the notice should be left at the **last known abode or place of business** of the other joint tenants, even if the notice is never read by the other joint tenant (**Kinch v Bullard (1999)**). Indeed, even if the notice cannot later be found, but on balance of probabilities was probably executed, then severance will have been deemed to have occurred, especially where the surrounding circumstances support severance (**Dunbabin v Dunbabin (2022)**). In *Dunbabin*, evidence of legal advice the parties had taken, together with the preparation of mirror wills purporting to leave the *shares separately*, was sufficient evidence.

10.33 In **Re 88 Berkley Road (1971)**, joint tenants shared a house. One of the two sought to serve a letter of written notice by recorded delivery. The letter was delivered, but it was not signed for by the intended joint tenant, rather by the joint tenant who had *served* the notice! The person who served the notice then died, and the surviving joint tenant tried to say that severance had not taken place so they could benefit from survivorship. However, the court said that delivery had taken place and that the joint tenancy severed.

10.34 Note that **service should be made on all the other joint tenants**. It is not necessary to serve a section 36(2) notice on anyone who happens to be a tenant in common. If a section 36(2) notice is returned to sender undelivered, severance by written notice will not have been effective (**Fantini (as executor of the estate of Iris Mary Fantini v Scrutton ((2020))**).

2. Common law methods ('such other acts or things')

10.35 This is the common law set down in the case of **Williams**

v Hensman (1861) and preserved by statute in s36(2), LPA 1925. The such other acts or things are:

(i)   An act operating on its share;

(ii) Mutual agreement;

(iii) Mutual conduct.

(i) Act operating on its share

10.36   This is an act which operates on the interest of a joint tenant *alone*. Under this method, **there is no need to inform the other joint tenants**. Where a joint tenant becomes bankrupt (**involuntary alienation**), this severs their interest (**Re Gorman (1990)**), and their interest vests in a trustee in bankruptcy. Mortgaging (**partial alienation**) an equitable interest also severs the joint tenancy (**Bedson v Bedson (1965); First National Security v Hegerty (1965)**). Finally, a sale or gift of the joint tenant's interest (**total alienation**), will sever the joint tenancy (**Brown v Raindle (1796)**). The interest can be transferred to anyone, even one of the other joint tenants. Even if the interest is transferred to another of the joint tenants, it will still be severed and will not re-merge with the joint tenancy.

(ii) Mutual agreement

10.37   Under this method of severance, **all joint tenants** must reach an **agreement to sever**. The agreement has no need to reach any particular formality, and in the case of **Burgess v Rawnsley (1975)(CA)**, the agreement to sell was entirely oral. It does not have to be a specifically enforceable contract (**Hunter v Babbage (1994)**). However, it is clear that mere negotiations are not sufficient to effect severance by this method (**Gore and Snell v Carpenter (1990); Neilson-Jones v Fedden (1974)**). This is because things change during the course of a negotiation.

(iii) Mutual conduct / 'course of dealing'

10.38   Under this method of severance, though the parties fail to reach agreement as to severance, their conduct is such that the joint tenancy is severed by the conduct. Severance by mutual conduct is rare and, indeed, the case law can sometimes overlap the two (see the judgment of Lord Denning MR in **Burgess v Rawnsley (1977)**).

10.39   Physical separation of the land by partition is not sufficient to effect severance of a joint tenancy *unless* there is evidence that the parties' mutual intention is that the joint tenancy should end (**Greenfield v Greenfield (1970)**). However, you should proceed with caution as such claims are likely to be fact-sensitive.

10.40   An accepted method of severance by mutual conduct is partition, which is, for example, separating one large parcel of land into two separate and distinct parcels of freehold. An order to this effect was made in **Ellison v Cleghorn (2013)**, where the intention had always been to segregate the titles from the outset when each joint owner was ready to build their own house.

3.   Forfeiture as a means of severance

10.41   What if one joint tenant unlawfully kills another joint tenant in order to take the benefit of survivorship? Will the law allow that? I would hope that your instinct is to say, 'No', because your instinct would be right. Public policy dictates, as expressed in section 1, Forfeiture Act 1982, that where one joint tenant is responsible for the death by unlawful killing of another joint tenant, the joint tenancy is severed and the right of survivorship does not operate.

10.42   The estate of the deceased person need only prove their case by the civil standard of proof, and there is no need for a criminal conviction in order for the case to proceed.

10.43   The harshness of the rule is understandable, but it is modified to allow flexibility where the *justice of the case* would require it. For example, in the case of **Re K (deceased) (1985)**, a husband and wife were joint tenants of the matrimonial home.

After a sustained period of domestic abuse committed by the husband against the wife, the wife killed the husband. Ordinarily, this would have severed the joint tenancy, but the court used the statutory power under section 2(1), Forfeiture Act 1982 to provide relief to the wife.

Co-ownership – The Modern Statutory Framework

10.44 We looked in chapter eight at the statutory regulation of common ownership under the Trusts of Land and Appointment of Trustees Act ('ToLATA') 1996, and we return to it now when considering how an end to the common ownership situation might be brought about.

10.45 Under s6, ToLATA 1996, the trustees under co-owned land have all the powers in dealing with the land of absolute owners. However, trustees remain subject to the rules of equity and the limitations placed on their actions by ToLATA 1996 where they are under an obligation to exercise their powers having regard to the rights of the beneficiaries (s6(5), ToLATA 1996). Additionally, the trustees are subject to the duty imposed by s1, Trustee Act 2000 to **exercise reasonable care and skill**.

10.46 In addition to these broad principles under ToLATA 1996, the Act is designed to settle disputes between co-owners as to sale of the land. Under ToLATA 1996, all land which is co-owned is held under a trust of land. However, under the old law, there was a presumption that land should be sold where there was a dispute as to sale.

10.47 ToLATA 1996 creates no obligation to sell, but does give the *power* to any interested party to seek an order for sale. Where the trustees seek sale of the property to divide the proceeds between the beneficiaries, they must carry out consultation with the beneficiaries of full age and beneficially entitled to an interest in possession in the land (s11(1), ToLATA 1996) and, give effect to the wishes of the beneficiaries, or the majority (by value) where there is a dispute.

Resolving a Dispute in Court – ss14, 15 ToLATA 1996 and s335A, Insolvency Act 1986

10.48 Where there are disputes as to sale that cannot be resolved by the parties, then an application can be made to court. Under section 14, ToLATA 1996, **any person with an interest**, eg, trustee, beneficiary, mortgagee (lender), or, trustee in bankruptcy, might make an application.

10.49 Under section 14, ToLATA 1996, the court may make **any order** relating to the trustees' exercise of their functions, meaning, the court may make an order for sale or confirm the trustees must postpone sale until the occurrence of a specified event or may also make an order relieving them of any obligation to obtain the consent of or to consult any person in connection with the exercise of their functions (s14(2), ToLATA 1996). However, the most common form of s14 application will be an order for sale.

10.50 Where an order for sale is sought by a beneficiary or a trustee, the court must take account of the guidelines in s15, ToLATA 1996. Where the application is by the trustee in bankruptcy, the court must consider the guidelines under s335A, Insolvency Act 1986.

s15, ToLATA 1996

10.51 The criteria under s15(3), ToLATA 1996 are:

(a) the intentions of the person(s) who created the trust;

(b) the purposes for which the trust property is to be held. For example, if the purpose endures, sale will not be ordered (**Re Buchanan-Wollaston's Conveyance (1939)**).

(c) the welfare of any minor who occupies or might reasonably be expected to occupy any land as his home;

(d) the interests of any secured creditor of any beneficiary.

10.52 Under s15(3), ToLATA, the circumstances and wishes of any beneficiaries of full age and, in dispute, those of the majority are also considered. It is also the case that the factors in section 15,

ToLATA 1996 do not have an hierarchy. In other words, (d) is given the same weight as (a) (**Mortgage Corporation v Shaire (2001)**). Importantly, the statute allows the court to adopt a flexible approach to each case, and *Shaire* is a good example of this flexibility.

10.53 In the case of *Shaire*, a couple owned a property in their joint names. The man, without the woman's knowledge, mortgaged the house twice by forging her signature. The man stopped paying the mortgage and then died. The mortgagee sought an order for sale under section 14. The woman resisted the order for sale. The mortgagee had a 25% interest in the property, while the woman held 75%. Rather than grant an order for sale, the court allowed repayment of the mortgage as a secured loan at three per cent above the bank base rate. This was, effectively, a compromise decision between the parties. The woman wanted to stay, whereas the mortgagee wanted the money tied up in its interest. By allowing repayment of the loan, the case struck a balance between the competing interests of the parties.

Cases on sections 14 and 15, ToLATA

10.54 It is useful to know the cases on section 14 applications and how the courts have used the section 15 criteria.

Case	Description
Edwards v Lloyds TSB (2004)	Co-owned property as family home, two parents and two children – Forged mortgage by husband – Relationship broke down – Mortgagee sought order for sale – Wife resisted on basis that she remained there with her young children – Court refused sale, allowed the wife and children to remain until youngest was 18 – Enough equity in house so security enforced later.
C. Putnam & Sons v Taylor (2009)	Co-owned family home – husband in debt – sale granted despite wife and children still living in house, ie, the purpose remained – Court satisfied wife had enough equity from sale to buy another house.
Edwards v	Co-owned home – Wife forged husband's signature to

Edwards & Bank of Scotland (2010)	obtain mortgage – Marriage ended – purpose of house purchase (matrimonial home) had come to an end – Sale order – Husband had enough equity to buy another house.
Fred Perry Ltd v Genis (2014)	Husband sole legal owner – three mortgages – Default on payments – Wife resisted order for sale – still lived there with two (minor) children – Sale ordered, but postponed for 12 months while new house and schools could be found.

s335A, Insolvency Act 1986

10.55   Where one of the co-owners is bankrupt, a different scheme applies. When a co-owner becomes bankrupt, their estate, meaning their property, including an interest which they have in land, vests in the trustee in bankruptcy. These means that someone else controls their property.

10.56   The trustee in bankruptcy makes the application under section 14, but the court does not consider the section 15 criteria, because it is a trustee in bankruptcy making the application, rather the court is directed to consider the criteria under section 335A, Insolvency Act 1986. This provision states that the court shall make such order as it thinks just and reasonable having regard to:

(a) the interests of the bankrupt's creditors;

(b) where the application is in respect of land that includes a dwelling house which is or has been the home of the bankrupt, his spouse or former spouse, the following criteria are taken into account:

(i) the conduct of the spouse or former spouse in so far as contributing to the bankruptcy;

(ii) the needs and financial resources of the spouse or former spouse; and

(iii) the needs of any children; and,

(c) all the circumstances of the case other than the needs of the bankrupt.

10.57 Criteria (b) and (c) can no longer be considered by the court after one year from bankruptcy, *unless the circumstances are exceptional*. After this period the interests of the bankrupt's creditors outweigh all other considerations. This raises the question of *what amounts to an exceptional circumstance?*

10.58 What amounts to an exceptional circumstance must vary from case to case, but guidance might be taken from some cases decided under the provision. In **Re Citro (1991)**, forcing a wife and children to leave the family home was not exceptional, but displacing a party with mental illness (schizophrenia), would be (**Re Raval (1998)**). Likewise, an applicant with terminal cancer and only a limited time to live was deemed exceptional (**Re Bremner (1999)**).

10.59 If something is part of the typical ups and downs of life, like moving house and moving children to another school, that is not likely to be regarded as exceptional.

CHAPTER 11
LEASES

Introduction

11.01   We have already looked at the characteristics of leases and how they are protected and binding on third parties in chapter two, paras 2.23 – 2.37 (inclusive). You may want to refresh your memory of this before reading this chapter.

11.02   Now, on the subject of this chapter, we cover a lot of ground here. Essentially, we cover:

(a) Types of Leases
(b) Lease / Licence Distinction
(c) Covenants in Leases
(d) Running of Leasehold Covenants
(e) Remedies and Termination of Leases

11.03   As I said, this is a lot of ground but that is because leases is such a large and important part of land law. I can make an educated guess that leases could be up to a third of your land law course, and some of you may even be doing specialist courses on landlord and tenant. Yes, it is such a big area of law that it could merit such a course.

(a) Types of Leases

11.04   As we saw in chapter two, leases have to satisfy certain conditions in order to be valid. Broadly, they have to have the **characteristics of a lease** (certain term, exclusive possession, (*maybe*) rent), satisfy the **correct formalities for the creation of a lease** (eg, a legal lease of more than three years must be by deed), and then the lease must be **protected in the correct way**. For example, the legal lease of more than seven years must be substantively registered. So far, so good, but within the umbrella concept of 'the lease', there is a range of **types of lease** you need to be aware of to make your understanding complete. So now, with that in mind, it's time for another table.

Lease Name	Description
Fixed Term Lease	This is a lease for a fixed period of time and comes to an end at the end of the fixed period. The lease will start and end on a fixed date.
Periodic Tenancy	Length of the term is *not* fixed, but it can still be certain as it will run from period to period. The relevant period is worked out on the rent calculation, not when the rent is paid by the tenant. For example, a tenant whose rent is calculated at £12,000 per year, payable every three months (quarterly), has an **annual periodic tenancy** because the rent is *calculated annually* **(Ladies' Hosiery and Underwear Ltd v Parker (1930))**. A periodic tenancy can be express or implied **(Prudential Assurance Co Ltd v London Residuary Body (1992))**. The *period* is a certain term.
Tenancy at Will	This arises where the tenant occupies land with the landlord's consent. Either party may terminate the tenancy at any time. The term is certain because it is worked out by the period of rent payment, eg, weekly, monthly, etc.
Tenancy at Sufferance	Tenant remains in possession, after original lease comes to an end, without the landlord's consent. The term is certain because it is worked out by the period of rent payment, eg, weekly, monthly, etc. Where the landlord subsequently consents, a tenancy at will may arise.

Tenancy by Estoppel	This tenancy arises where the elements of proprietary estoppel are satisfied. The *landlord* will be stopped from denying a lease in those circumstances.
Tenancy for Life	A tenancy granted for life is converted by statute into a tenancy for a fixed term of 90 years (s149(6) LPA 1925).

11.05   Before moving to the next part, something should be said about the odd House of Lords case of **Bruton v London & Quadrant Housing Trust (2000)** because it raises an interesting *hybrid* form of lease. In *Bruton*, Lambeth Borough Council granted a licence over flats it owned to London & Quadrant Housing Trust ('Quadrant'). Quadrant used the flats to provide accommodation to homeless people. Bruton was given exclusive possession of one of the flats under a 'licence to occupy'. The flat needed repairs and Bruton argued that, as a tenant, the landlord was under an obligation to repair under s11, Landlord and Tenant Act 1985. Quadrant argued that Bruton was a mere licencee, so the section 11 obligation did not apply to them.

11.06   The House of Lords held that Bruton was a tenant. The elements of a lease were satisfied (certain term, exclusive possession, and rent), so Quadrant was liable for the repairs under the statutory duty. Now, I said that the decision was odd. Well, the odd part is that Lambeth BC gave Quadrant a licence to occupy the flats, but the House of Lords said that what Quadrant was giving was a lease. Effectively, therefore, Quadrant was giving to occupants more (a lease) than they had themselves (a licence). Remember, a lease is a property right capable of binding third parties, but a licence is a personal right *not* capable of binding third parties.

11.07   So, what is this interest? Well, it is not quite a proprietary interest since it did not bind Lambeth BC. Essentially, it was a **non-proprietary lease** binding only on the parties to the agreement, namely Bruton and Quadrant. The case of *Bruton* was applied in **Islington LBC v Green (2005)** and **Kay v Lambeth LBC (2006)**, both cases re-asserting the non-proprietary nature of the lease.

(b) Lease / Licence Distinction

11.08   This area of law is not as important or significant as it was 30-odd years ago, but it still seems to pop-up from time-to-time in law courses up and down the country. So, I cover it here under sufferance (pun very much intended). What is the issue?

11.09   The holder of a lease gets certain rights which the holder of a licence does not get. A lease, as you know, is a proprietary interest capable of binding third parties, whereas a licence is a personal right which does not bind third parties. Further, a holder of certain types of lease can enforce a repairing obligation against a landlord, and seek certain reliefs if a landlord seeks to forfeit a lease. So, there is some value in establishing a lease over a licence, even today. However, the main protections tenants enjoyed historically, that is, rent control (that rent could not increase too much) and security of tenure (that a tenant could stay after the fixed term ended), have been all but removed in private tenancies since the Rent Act 1977 was repealed in the 1980s. Nevertheless, the courts are still troubled, through less frequently, by cases concerned with the lease/licence distinction.

11.10   The main area of contention in the lease/licence distinction was in relation to the issue of exclusive possession. You will recall, that exclusive possession gives the leaseholder the right to exclude everyone from the land, including the landlord. In this context, landlords would try to introduce terms into the agreement to undermine the right to exclusive possession and, thus, ensure that what was created was not a lease, but a licence.

11.11   Landlords could attempt to undermine exclusive possession by such as retention of a key to gain unfettered access to the land; provide services to the tenant, such as cleaning services and the provision of clean linen. Alternatively, that there was no intention to create legal relations and, as such, there was no lease. Let's consider these scenarios.

Issue	Case Law
Key	Landlords retain keys for access, so there is no magic in a key (**Aslan v Murphy (1990)**). The importance of a key will depend on the reason for retention and, if for some spurious reason, eg, to gain access from 1030am – midday each day to let others share the room, then the court is likely to regard it as a sham not undermining exclusive possession.
Cleaning Services and Linen	The provision of services by the landlord may create a licence, not a lease. The question is whether the provision of services is genuine or a sham (**Marchant v Charters (1977); Markou v Da Silvaesa (1986)**).
Intention to Create Legal Relations ('ICLR')	If there is no ICLR, then there will be no lease. Generally, arrangements with family, friendship, and non-commercial contexts will not have a lease because of a lack of ICLR (**Facchini v Bryson (1952)**), though a family context will not be enough on its own to find there is no ICLR. The courts will look at the arrangement to see what it genuinely looks to create (**Nunn v Dalrymple (1990)**).
Service Occupancy	Some forms of employment provide accommodation as part of the work, so that the employee is near the workplace and able to perform their tasks more easily. In such circumstances, it is more likely to be a licence to occupy, not a lease. (**Norris v Checksfield (1991)**). Where the accommodation is incidental to the work, a tenancy is more likely to be found (**Royal Philanthropic Society v County (1985)**).
Introducing Others	The *landlord* retaining the power to introduce additional people to the accommodation may be genuine, and therefore create a licence, but if a sham clause, then it is more likely to be a lease. In **AG Securities v Vaughan (1990)**, four rooms let separately to different people at different times on different agreements was not a lease but a licence to occupy. By contrast, in Antoniades v Villiers (1990), a co-habiting couple agreed to rent a one-bedroom flat

	with a double bed. The *landlord* retained the right to allow new people to share the flat. The court said this was a sham. The reality is that a one-bedroom flat could not be shared with new people, especially where the occupants were a couple. Therefore, the couple had a lease, no matter how hard the landlord tried to say it was a licence.

(c) Covenants in Leases

11.12   The covenants in a lease are the obligations which the landlord and tenant each agree will be binding for the length of the lease. These covenants can be positive or negative, express or implied, and they can vary significantly from lease to lease.

11.13   Typical covenants include the **tenant's covenant to pay rent to the landlord,** or a covenant **not to use a residential premises for business purposes**. Generally, covenants are split into those which the landlord agrees to perform, and those which the tenant agrees to perform.

Landlord's Covenants

Quiet Enjoyment

11.14   A landlord agrees that the tenant should have **quiet enjoyment** of the premises for the length of the lease. This may be express or implied, and means that the landlord will allow the tenant possession of the premises, without interference from the landlord, for the duration of the lease (**Kenny v Preen (1963)**). In **Owen v Gadd (1956)**, the landlord was liable for erecting scaffolding around the premises which prevented the tenant from gaining access, while in **Lavender v Betts (1942)** removal of a door was a breach of this covenant.

No derogation from grant

11.15   Once the lease has been granted, the landlord should not do something which would be inconsistent with the grant of the lease. In **Aldin v Latimer Clark Muirhead & Co (1894)**, a lease was taken for the purpose of using the premises for drying out timber, but the landlord was held to have derogated from grant by erecting buildings around the leased premises which interrupted the air flow needed to dry the tenant's timber.

Fitness for Human Habitation

11.16 A landlord is *generally* **not** under an obligation to let premises which are fit for human habitation (**Lane v Cox (1897)**), unless the premises has been let fully furnished, in which case it must be for human habitation at the start of the lease (**Wilson v Finch Hatton (1877)**).

11.17 However, the position at common law must now be read in light of the Homes (Fitness for Human Habitation) Act 2018 which creates a new right for tenants. The right is engaged where the landlord has failed to maintain the leased premises which is a dwelling house to an appropriate standard. The 2018 Act amends sections 8 – 10, inclusive, of the Landlord and Tenant Act 1985.

11.18 The 2018 Act implies into some tenancies that the dwelling house must be fit for human habitation at the start of the tenancy, and that it remains fit for human habitation for the duration of the tenancy.

Repair

11.19 A covenant to repair can, as a rule, be conferred on either party to a lease (**Cavalier v Pope (1906)**), but there is an exception for **leases of not more than seven years**. In such circumstances, ss 11 – 14, Landlord and Tenant Act 1985, impose a maintenance and repair obligation on the landlord. This relates to the structure and exterior of the building, and to keep utilities installations in repair, namely, water supply, gas, electricity, sanitation, etc. The lease cannot purport to exclude s 11, Landlord and Tenant Act 1985.

11.20 The repair obligation is engaged where the landlord is aware of the disrepair, usually by the tenant informing the landlord (**O'Brien v Robinson (1973)**). Further, the disrepair should be something for which the landlord can be reasonably responsible, so condensation damaging the interior of a house due to a design fault in the windows was not something which fell under the section 11 of the 1985 Act (**Lee v Leeds City Council (2002)**). It should be noted that actions only lie in respect of a breach of section 11 of the 1985 Act where the applicant occupies the land as a tenant and not as a licensee (**Khan v Mehmood (2022)**).

Tenant's Covenants

Rates and Taxes

11.21   The tenant is under an implied obligation to pay rates and taxes which fall due on the leased premises.

Damage or disrepair

11.22   Tenants are under an obligation **not to commit waste**, meaning the tenant must avoid acts which alter the state of the land. **Voluntary waste** is something done deliberately to alter the land, eg, demolishing an internal wall. **Permissive waste** is something being left so that the premises is damaged. Linked to this is the obligation to **use the premises in a tenant-like manner** (**Warren v Keen (1954)**).

Permitting the landlord access

11.23   The tenant should permit the landlord access to the premises to carry out repairs on the premises (**McGreal v Wake (1984)**).

Alienation clauses

11.24   A landlord can sometimes place restrictions on the ability of the tenant to assign or sub-let the premises. An assignment is the transfer the whole of the remainder of the lease to another so there is a new tenant. A sub-let is the creation of a new tenancy for a period shorter than the tenant's term. The holder of the short lease term is known as the sub-tenant.

11.25 Landlords typically restrict such actions by the tenant because the landlord would not necessarily have a chance to assess whether the assignee or sub-tenant will be a good tenant of the property.

11.26 Such clauses can be absolute or, as is more common, qualified. The qualification is that the tenant seeks the landlord's consent before the assignment or sub-let. Under section 19, Landlord and Tenant Act 1927, the landlord's consent to an assignment cannot be unreasonably withheld.

11.27 Under section 1(3), Landlord and Tenant Act 1988, upon where a landlord receives a written request for consent, the landlord is under a duty to consent within a reasonable time unless they have a reasonable reason for withholding consent. Where consent is withheld, the landlord must write giving reasons. The landlord has the burden of proving refusal is reasonable (section 1(6), Landlord and Tenant Act 1988.

11.28 The difficulty here is what amounts to 'reasonable' for the purposes of refusing consent to assignment or sub-let. There is guidance provided by **International Drilling Fluids Ltd v Louisville Investment Ltd (1986)**:

(a) What is the purpose of the qualified covenant against assignment? Is it to keep undesirable activity off the landlord's land?
(b) Landlord cannot refuse consent to matters unrelated to the relationship of landlord and tenant.
(c) Landlord only needs to satisfy that the conclusions would have been reached by a reasonable person in the circumstances.
(d) May be reasonable to refuse consent for a purpose, even though not prohibited in the lease.
(e) The landlord should grant or withhold consent on grounds of proportionality, from the perspective of both the

landlord and the tenant.

(f) Remember, each case will turn on its facts, and reasonableness may depend on the circumstances.

(d) Running of Leasehold Covenants

11.29   What happens if the landlord sells their land (this is known as the **freehold reversion**) which is subject to a lease? Can the new owner enforce covenants against the tenant, or be liable for breach of the landlord's covenants? Alternatively, what happens if the tenant transfers (this is known as **assignment** or **assigning**) the lease to a new tenant? Can the new tenant enforce covenants which the landlord might have breached, and be held to covenants which the previous tenant agreed? Well, the short answer is that it depends on satisfaction of various rules, and when the lease in question was first granted. The **date the lease was first granted is important** because that will determine whether the **'old rules'** or the **'new rules'** apply to it. Let's start with the 'old rules'.

'Old rules'

11.30   For a lease which was granted before 1st January 1996, the 'old rules' apply. These rules are a mixture of common law and statute.

11.31   The starting point is to say that **all covenants agreed between the original landlord and the original tenant are enforceable between them as a matter of contract**, namely, the doctrine of privity of contract operates to make the enforceable. This includes personal as well as proprietary covenants. However, when either the freehold reversion or the lease change hands, only proprietary covenants are potentially enforceable.

'Old rules' – Landlord's sale of freehold reversion

11.32   Under **ss141** and **142, Law of Property Act 1925**, the benefit (s141) and the burden (s142) of the original lease, are enforceable by, and against, the new owner of the freehold reversion, provided it has **reference to the subject-matter of the lease**, meaning that the covenant is proprietary.

11.33   One slight quirk of these provisions is that the seller loses all his rights to enforce breaches of covenant which occurred while he was in possession, and they pass, instead, to the new landlord (**Re King (1963)**), including the right to sue for any unpaid rent (**Arlesford Trading Company Ltd v Servansingh (1971)**).

11.34   A further quirk of the old law is that the original tenant can enforce the lessor's covenants against the original landlord, even though the original landlord has sold the freehold reversion (**Stuart v Joy (1904)**). This is because of the **doctrine of privity of contract**.

'Old rules' – sub-tenants

11.35   What if the tenant sub-lets the property? In other words, they retain the main lease, but grant a third party a lease of a shorter period than their own. Can the main landlord (known as the 'head landlord') sue the sub-tenant for breaches of covenant which were agreed by the original tenant? Generally, the answer is 'no'. Why? Well, this is because there is no **privity of contract** between the head landlord and the sub-tenant, ie, they have no direct contractual relationship. Further, there is also no **privity of estate** between the head landlord and the sub-tenant.

11.36   However, though the answer is generally, 'no', there are exceptions: (i) Indirect enforcement; (ii) Restrictive covenants in the head lease.

(i)   Indirect enforcement

11.37   This is achieved by the head landlord suing the original tenant who, in turn, sues the sub-tenant. The reason the tenant can be sued is because they are responsible for the breaches committed by a sub-tenant under **s79, LPA 1925**.

(ii)   Restrictive covenants in the head lease

11.38   Where the covenant is restrictive, eg, states that a residential premises may not be used for business purposes, the **landlord may enforce the covenant directly against the sub-tenant (Hemingway Securities Ltd v Dunraven Ltd (1995))**. The conditions are taken from the case of **Tulk v Moxhay (1848)**, which is the case on enforceability of restrictive covenants in freehold land. You can look again at the detail in chapter four, paragraphs 4.29 – 4.35 (inclusive), but as a memory-refresher, these are:

(i)   The covenant must be negative in substance;

(ii)   The covenant must accommodate the dominant tenement;

(iii) The original parties must have intended that the burden should bind successors;

(iv) The person against whom the covenant is being enforced must have notice of it.

'Old rules' – Tenants assignment of the lease

11.39   The transfer of a lease (known as an assignment) to a new tenant will allow covenants to be enforced provided certain conditions are satisfied. The conditions for enforcement are:

(i)   There must be privity of estate, ie, a relationship of current landlord and current tenant;

(ii)   It must be a legal lease;

(iii) The legal lease must have been legally assigned; AND,

(iv) The leasehold covenant must touch and concern the land.

(i)   There must be privity of estate, ie, a relationship of current landlord and current tenant

11.40   There is **privity of estate** where there is a relationship of **current landlord and current tenant** between the landlord and the new tenant. This is easily satisfied.

(ii)   It must be a legal lease

11.41   Where the lease has been created by deed and protected in the correct manner, or falls within the exception in s54(2), LPA 1925, the lease will be legal (**Boyer v Warby (1953)**).

(iii)   The legal lease must have been legally assigned

11.42   A legal lease is legally assigned by using a deed (s52 LPA 1925), which is a document which complies with s1, LP(MP)A 1989, meaning it is written, states on its face it is a deed, is signed by the grantor, witnessed, and delivered (dated). The lease will then need to be registered in the appropriate way.

(iv)   The leasehold covenant must touch and concern the land

11.43   This is the requirement that the covenant is one which affects the land, not one which is merely personal to the landlord and tenant.

'Old rules' – Continuing liability of tenant after assignment

11.44   As stated earlier, the original landlord remains liable throughout the lease. It is also the case that the original tenant remains liable on covenants in a pre-1996 lease (**Allied London Ltd v Hambro Ltd (1984)**), even after assignment of the lease. Thus, the original tenant may be liable for breaches committed by the new tenant. In such circumstances, the original tenant may look for means of getting their money back from the new tenant. Fortunately, the original tenant does have some options.

11.45 First, they could rely on the **law of unjust enrichment** (**Moule v Garrett (1872)**) which requires that the original tenant be reimbursed by the new tenant for any costs incurred by the original tenant because the new tenant breached the leasehold covenants.

11.46 Secondly, the original tenant might rely on either **sch 12, para 20, Land Registration Act 2002**, which **implies an indemnity covenant** into the assignment of the lease, where title to the lease is registered, or a similar provision in **s77, Law of Property Act 1925**, where title to the lease is unregistered. An indemnity covenant effectively means that the new tenant agrees to pay the old tenant if the old tenant suffers loss for any breach the new tenant commits.

'New rules' – Landlord and Tenant (Covenants) Act 1995

11.47 This statute applies to **all leases granted on or after 1ˢᵗ January 1996**, and makes quite radical changes to the 'old rules', discussed above.

11.48 Under the 1995 Act, the **original tenant is automatically released from the burden of leasehold covenants when lease is assigned (s5, LT(C)A 1995)**. The landlord is not, however, automatically released from the burden of covenants, but may serve a notice of release (**s6, LT(C)A 1995**) on the tenant with a request, but this has been doubted by (**London Diocesan Fund v Avonridge Property Company Limited (2005)(HL)**).

11.49 Further, covenants **no longer** *need to touch and concern or have reference to the subject-matter of the lease* to pass (**ss2 and 3, LT(C)A 1995**). The **benefit and burden** of all leasehold covenants pass automatically on assignment of the lease or transfer of the freehold reversion, unless they are expressed to be personal (**First Penthouse v Channel Hotels and Properties (2003)**). It is also the case that the anomalous case of **Re King (1963)**, discussed at 11.33, above, is reversed for "new" leases (**s24(4), LT(C)A 1995**).

Authorised Guarantee Agreements ('AGA')

11.50   Though it is the case that under the LT(C)A 1995, the original tenant is released from the burden of covenants when they assign the lease, the landlord, as a condition of assignment, can require the new tenant to enter into an **authorised guarantee agreement** ('AGA') (**s16, LT(C)A 1995**). Under an AGA, the original tenant agrees to guarantee the performance, by the new tenant, of the covenants under the lease. If the lease is assigned again, the AGA agreed by the original tenant is **automatically discharged**.

11.51   A tenant may only enter into an AGA where the landlord demonstrates that there is a qualified or absolute prohibition on assignment in the lease and that any consent to assignment of the lease is given subject to the condition that the tenant assigning the lease enters into an AGA.

11.52   Merely entering into an AGA does not mean that the tenant is wholly exposed to the wrongdoing of the new tenant, since s17, LT(C)A 1995 states that the landlord must serve notice within six months of any unpaid rent becoming due, stating the amount owed. Any tenant who has to **pay the arrears of a new tenant has the right to be granted an overriding lease (s19, LT(C)A 1995)** for a **term equal to the remainder of the tenancy plus three days**. An overriding lease essentially allows the original (old) tenant to become the landlord of the current tenant, which gives the holder of the overriding lease the power to forfeit the lease and prevent other breaches by injunction.

11.53   These provisions of the LT(C)A 1995 are **retrospective**, and **apply to old leases and new leases**.

(e) Remedies and Termination

Tenant's Remedies for Landlord's Breach of Covenant

11.54   A tenant has a range of remedies available where a landlord is in breach of covenant. First, the tenant might claim an

injunction against the landlord which either prevents a threatened breach of trust (a **prohibitory injunction**), or forces the landlord to undertake repairs where, for example, they are under a statutory obligation to repair, as under s11, Landlord and Tenant Act 1985. An injunction which forces the landlord to do something is a **mandatory injunction**. As an alternative to a mandatory injunction, a tenant might also ask for the remedy of **specific performance** against the landlord. This equitable remedy requires an individual to perform the positive obligations under a lease. Importantly, **s17, Landlord and Tenant Act 1985** confirms that the remedies of mandatory injunction and specific performance are available in relation to the landlord's repairing obligation, but that the usual bars on equitable remedies do not operate.

11.55 Further remedies include a claim for **damages for breach of covenant**, which are assessed on the basis of the loss which the tenant has suffered, eg, from moving out and having to pay rent for alterative accommodation while repairs are carried out. Finally, the tenant may **repudiate** the lease, treating it as being at an end (**Hussein v Mehlman (1992)**).

Landlord's Remedies for Tenant's Breach of Covenant

11.56 The landlord's remedies available against the tenant vary depending on what covenant has been breached: whether the covenant is the rent, or the non-rent, covenant.

Remedies for non-payment of rent

11.57 If the tenant has not paid the rent, then the remedy of an **action for recovery of the debt** will be available. The ancient remedy of **distraint** was abolished by Part 3, Tribunals, Courts and Enforcement Act 2007, and replaced with a scheme to operate in relation to commercial leases only, namely the Commercial Rent Arrears Recovery scheme, which came into force on 6th April 2014.

11.58 Alternatively, a landlord may **forfeit the lease** for non-payment of rent. **Forfeiture**, is the remedy of the landlord **taking the lease back and bringing an end to the landlord and**

tenant relationship. In order to forfeit a lease, there must be a forfeiture clause in the lease; without one, the lease may not be forfeited. It may be achieved by **peaceful re-entry** of the premises, or by **court order**. Note, it may only be by court order where the premises is residential.

11.59 The tenant may seek relief from forfeiture, that is, they may seek to reverse the forfeiture action by the landlord. If under the jurisdiction of the County Court, then the tenant must make their application within six months of the date on which the landlord recovered possession (s138(9A), County Courts Act 1984), where possession was made by court order, or within six months of the date of the landlord taking possession (s139, CCA 1984) (**Golding v Martin (2019)(CA)**). If under the jurisdiction of the High Court, and forfeiture was by court order, an application must be made within six months of execution of the judgment (s38(1), Senior Courts Act 1981; s210, Common Law Procedure Act 1852). Where by peaceful re-entry, the court may grant relief under its inherent jurisdiction (**Billson v Residential Apartments (1992)(CA)**), but there is no set limitation period, but it is likely to be subject to any consideration of delay.

11.60 In October 2019, the Supreme Court in **Manchester Ship Canal Co Ltd v Vauxhall Motors Ltd**, held that it was possible to seek relief from forfeiture where something other than a proprietary right was held by the claimant. Thus, the Court permitted relief from forfeiture of a licence held by Vauxhall Motors Ltd.

Remedies for breach of non-rent covenants

11.61 A landlord may claim an injunction or specific performance against the tenant for breach of covenant, though specific performance is a rarely used remedy against a tenant from the landlord's perspective. Further, the landlord may also bring an action for damages against the tenant for breach of covenant, assessed on the basis of the loss which the landlord has suffered (18, Landlord and Tenant Act 1927; Leasehold Property (Repairs) Act 1938).

11.62 The landlord may also **forfeit** the lease from breach of a covenant other than a rent covenant. The procedure is provided in **s146, Law of Property Act 1925**, which requires that a notice be served:

(i) Specifying the breach which has occurred; and,

(ii) If capable of remedy, require that it be remedied within a reasonable time; and,

(iii) Require the tenant to pay compensation if required.

11.63 If the breach is not remedied, then the landlord may forfeit by **court order** or **peaceful re-entry**. Some breaches are incapable of remedy, such as those which place a taint on the land. For example, use of the leased premises for immoral purposes in **Governors of Rugby School v Tannahill (1935)** is not capable of remedy.

11.64 It should be noted that a right of re-entry must have arisen before a s146 notice is served (**Toms v Ruberry (2019)(CA)**).

11.65 The tenant may apply for discretionary relief from forfeiture under **s146(2), Law of Property Act 1925**. The exercise of the discretion will depend on the circumstances of the case.

Termination of a Lease

11.66 A lease may be terminated by the **passage of time**; the term simply comes to an end, or by a **break clause** contained in the lease which allows the landlord or tenant to bring the lease to a premature conclusion. Equally, a lease may come to an end by **surrender**, or by **merger**, as where the tenant acquires the freehold. Finally, as stated, it may also come to an end by **forfeiture**.

CHAPTER 12
ADVERSE POSSESSION

Introduction

12.01   As already indicated, while land law generally requires formality in the acquisition of estates and interests in land, in some circumstances estates and interests might be acquired informally. One instance is proprietary estoppel, which we considered in chapter seven. In this chapter we consider another, namely, **adverse possession**.

12.02   Like so much of land law, the law relating to adverse possession is a mixture of **common law rules** and **statutory rules**. The common law rules help to answer the question as to whether adverse possession has occurred, while the statutory rules provide us with time periods. This is because adverse possession will only occur, once the common law rules are satisfied, where the relevant statutory period of possession has been met. The period differs, as you will see, as to whether the title against which adverse possession is claimed is registered or unregistered and, for registered title, when the relevant period was complete.

12.03   Now, before we look at the common law rules, I want to make to get something on terminology out of the way. Throughout this chapter I will sometimes refer to the *true* owner as the **paper owner**. This is a reference back to when legal owners of title to land proved their ownership by having the paper deed as proof of ownership. This terminology continues to creep into discussion of adverse possession, so forgive me if that happens in this chapter, because it will do. Of course, as you know now, title is proved, for the most part, by registration, and proof by paper is less and less frequent. As for other terminology, the person claiming the land by adverse possession will be referred to as the squatter. Again, this terminology is a little outdated, but continues to crop up from time to time.

Definition

12.04 Let's start with the definition of adverse possession. Adverse possession occurs where through **dispossession** or **discontinuance**, a squatter takes **ordinary possession** of land for the **period required by law, without paper owner's consent**, and acquires title to the land by those actions. Note, some of these elements overlap.

12.05 As can be seen, the paper owner can be dispossessed by the squatter or discontinue their own possession. As to whether possession has occurred, the courts look to **factual possession** and the **intention to possess**.

Has possession occurred?

12.06 In order to show possession, the claimant must demonstrate:

(i) Factual possession (*factum possessionis*); AND,

(ii) Intention to possess (*animus possidendi*)

JA Pye (Oxford) Ltd v Graham (2003)(HL)

12.07 Though these are separate requirements, they overlap heavily and **intention can often be found** by looking at the **factual possession (JA Pye (Oxford) Ltd v Graham (2003)(HL))**. Indeed, the practical approach is to look at all the circumstances of the claim (**Smart v Lambeth BC (2013)(CA)**). Each requirement is, nevertheless, considered separately.

(i) Factual possession (factum possessionis)

12.08 The factual possession required must endure for the relevant period of adverse possession and whether it is successful will depend on the facts; it is truly fact sensitive. What is clear is that the squatter should, alone and not with others or the paper owner, exercise some physical control of the land. However, what amounts to physical control will vary depending on the nature of the land and the manner in which the land is commonly used. Here, it will be instructive to provide a table of the forms of activity which amount to factual possession:

Action	Case Law
Fencing	Fences are good evidence of adverse possession (**Seddon v Smith (1877)**; **Haandrikman v Heslam (2021)**), but they have to be for the exclusion of others and not merely to keep animals in (**Powell v McFarlane (1977)**; **Wimpey Ltd v Sohn (1967)**)! Repairing fences erected by another may be insufficient alone (**Boosey v Davis (1988)**), but repair, repainting, hedge trimming, and grass cutting may suffice (**Wallis's Cayton Bay Holiday Camp Ltd v Shell-Mex and BP Ltd (1975)**).
Gates and Padlocks	Placing a gate and ensuring it is locked, either with a standard locking mechanism or a padlock is good evidence of factual possession (**Buckinghamshire CC v Moran (1990)**; **Pye v Graham (2002)**), and the same is true of the front door to a flat where the removal of door and replacement of it and the locks would be enough (**Lambeth LBC v Blackburn (2001)**)
Building	The squatter preparing the land for building work (**Treloar v Nute (1977)**) would be enough, as would building.
Farming	Since a number of cases involve adverse possession of farmland, agricultural use of agricultural land is a good measure of factual possession. However, minor acts such as grazing and hay cutting are insufficient alone (**Powell v McFarlane (1977)**). Generally, more is needed, such as grazing, manuring, maintenance of boundary hedges and fences, and padlocking with the only retained key (**Pye v Graham (2002)**).
Security	Another measure of intention to possess to the exclusion of others would be providing security cameras and lighting (**Prudential Assurance Ltd v Waterloo Real Estate (1999)**).

12.09 In the recent case of **Thorpe v Frank (2019)(CA)**, the paving of an open area in front of a bungalow, without fencing around the entire area, was also sufficient factual possession, especially as the paving of the adversely possessed area matched that which the claimant already owned.

12.10 What the case law demonstrates is that the more substantial the activity, the more likely it is to amount to factual possession. It stands to reason, therefore, that minimal acts will not meet the necessary level of factual possession (**Hounslow LBC v Minchinton (1997)**).

(ii) Intention to possess (animus possidendi)

12.11 The squatter's intention needed is the **intention to possess**, *not* the intention to own (**Buckinghamshire CC v Moran (1990)**). Part of that intention is the exclusion of the whole world, including the actual owner (**Powell v McFarlane (1977)**), which point was affirmed by the Court of Appeal in **White v Amirtharaja (2022)**.

12.12 As it is intention to possess, it does not matter that the squatter does not intend to remain permanently on the land, though they must complete the relevant period of adverse possession. It is also the case that neither the squatter having knowledge of the paper owner's future intentions with the property, eg, to sell for development, or that the squatter is willing to leave should the owner seek to take back possession, will undermine an intention to possess (**Buckinghamshire CC v Moran (1990); Pye v Graham (2002)**).

12.13 Quite often, intention can be inferred from the conduct of the person in possession. As stated earlier, there can be overlap between intention and factual possession, and drawing intention from conduct is an instance of that.

12.14 One thing is clear, namely that the intention to possess must be clear, so that anyone observing the possession, even the owner, would grasp that someone else was in possession of the land (**Powell v McFarlane (1977)**).

12.15 Naturally, anything which is contrary to the intention to possess will work against the squatter. Therefore, holding a right under a lease or a licence will undermine the claim (**BP Properties v Buckler (1987)**), as will acknowledgement that someone has a better title than you claim (**Lambeth LBC v Archangel (2002)**). However, a willingness to accept a licence or to pay rent, if challenged, will not defeat the claim (**JA Pye (Oxford) Ltd v Graham (2003)(HL)**).

12.16 It is also the case that the simple act of storage of items in an area was insufficient to demonstrate intention to dispossess, especially where the storage was exercised in accordance with an easement (**Littledale v Liverpool College (1900)**).

12.17 It follows from this that for the paper owner to defeat the squatter's claim to adverse possession, the paper owner must bring proceedings to remove the squatter and recover possession of the land.

The Clock

12.18 Once the elements of adverse possession have been satisfied, the squatter must demonstrate that they have been in possession of the land for the correct length of time. Generally, this will depend on whether title to the land is registered or unregistered. There are three schemes:

    (i)   adverse possession where title is unregistered;

    (ii) adverse possession of registered title under the old law;

    (iii) adverse possession of registered title under the new law.

12.19 Before we consider those three, it should be noted at what point the clock starts to 'tick'. Well, it starts once the owner has been dispossessed, or abandoned possession.

(i)   adverse possession where title is unregistered

12.20   The period of adverse possess in unregistered title is 12 years continuous possession (s15(1), Limitation Act 1980), and the clock runs from the moment of adverse possession. After the requisite period is complete, the owner's title is extinguished, and the adverse possessor's title is superior (**Buckinghamshire CC v Moran (1990)**).

12.21   The successful possessor does, however, take the property subject to all pre-existing legal and equitable rights, whether registered under Land Charges Act 1972 or not.

12.22   If the title possessed is a leasehold, the extinguishing of title relates only to the tenant's estate, not the landlord's estate.

(ii)   adverse possession of registered title under the old law

12.23   If the title possessed is registered and the period of 12 years continuous possession was completed before 13th October 2003, then that will satisfy the old law. Now, you may think that this is less and less relevant as the years go on, but successful claims under the old law of adverse possession do pop up from time to time, and there was a successful one recently (**Calverley Village Day Nursery Ltd v Lynch and another (2022)**).

12.24   If successful, the squatter would be entitled to entered on the register as proprietor and the paper owner held the property on trust until registration.

(iii)   adverse possession of registered title under the new law

12.25   The modern scheme of adverse possession where title is registered is to be found in the Land Registration Act 2002. The new law makes it more difficult to obtain a registered title by adverse possession.

12.26   First, there is no automatic limitation period, therefore **no loss of title merely by passage of a fixed period of time** (s96, LRA 2002), even if the claimant is able to show factual possession and an intention to possess. What happens now is governed by schedule 6, LRA 2002. After 10 years, a claimant may apply to be registered and if the Registrar thinks there is an arguable case for registration, notification is sent to the current registered proprietor (sch 6, para 2, LRA 2002).

12.27   Once the notice is received, the registered owner may **consent**, **object**, or **serve a counter-notice**.

12.28   Where the paper owner **consents**, the squatter will be registered as the proprietor of the estate after 65 days.

12.29   Where the paper owner **objects**, it should be in writing and signed giving reasons for objection to the squatter's registration. The nature of the objection is that the squatter has not satisfied the common law rules on adverse possession.

12.30   Finally, a **counter-notice** operates as follows. The paper owner accepts the common law elements of adverse possession have been made, but that they wish to assert their superior title. It is worth noting that the paper owner may object *and* issue a counter-notice.

12.31   Where the paper owner files a counter-notice, the squatter's application for registration of title is rejected unless the squatter, in their application, relies on one of the exceptions listed in schedule 6, paragraph 5. These exceptions are: estoppel, some other reason, and a boundary dispute.

12.32   The purpose of the **estoppel exception** relates to the notion of objection by the paper owner being unconscionable because of the squatter placing detrimental reliance on some assurance made by the paper owner.

12.33   The **other reason exception** relates to the fact that the squatter may contend that they have taken title following the death of a proprietor, or where there was an exchange of contracts on which the squatter paid an agreed purchase price.

12.34   The boundary dispute exception almost speaks for itself, but relates to those circumstances where the boundary of the property is incorrectly marked because of a fence or wall being placed on the incorrect line. The exception will only operate where the dispute relates to land in the area of the general boundary between the applicant's land and the registered proprietor's land (**Dowse and another v City of Bradford Metropolitan District Council (2020)**).

12.35 Where the squatter's application for registration as proprietor is rejected, the paper owner has a further two years to evict the squatter. If the paper owner takes no action for the further two years, and the squatter makes a further application to be registered as the proprietor, then the paper owner will not be able to provide objection or issue a counter-notice.

12.36 One final point about adverse possession. Since the coming into force of section 144, Legal Aid, Sentencing and Punishment of Offenders Act 2012, a criminal offence has been created in relation to residential buildings. The offence applies where:

- a person is in a residential building as a trespasser having entered it as a trespasser

- the person knows or ought to know that he or she is a trespasser, and

- the person is living in the building or intends to live there for any period

12.37 In **Best v Chief Land Registrar (2015)(CA)**, the court was clear that the provision criminalises trespass in residential buildings without affecting the operation of adverse possession.

ABOUT THE AUTHOR

I'm a law lecturer with 25 years' experience of teaching and explaining the law at undergraduate and postgraduate levels. I have tutored students in both the public and private sectors, at old and new universities, across a range of subjects, including land law.

Printed in Great Britain
by Amazon

42952760R00096